WHAT'S FOREVER FOR?

All the best Matt, PleAse stay
in touch

Blessings.
Dr. Jeep

WHAT'S FOREVER FOR?

A Physician's Guide for Everlasting
Love and Success in Marriage

DR. GEORGE "JEEP" NAUM

FAMILY PHYSICIAN AND MARITAL COACH

purposely
created
PUBLISHING

WHAT'S FOREVER FOR?
Published by Purposely Created Publishing Group™
Copyright © 2020 George "Jeep" Naum
All rights reserved.

Printed in the United States of America

ISBN: 978-1-64484-263-8

TABLE OF CONTENTS

INTRODUCTION

To say the least, my wife and I have had a blessed marriage. Our marriage truly has been a gift from God, and it has been what I imagined a marriage to be in every way. We have worked at it very hard. Besides God, our marriage is first in our lives.

In my career as a physician, I have seen many marriages die on the vine. It has always been very sad for me to see that happen.

Recently, through a plethora of trials and tribulations, my life has taken a very different path and I have made it my mission to try and help as many people as I can to not only prevent problems in their marriages, but to help resurrect failing marriages so that couples can become best friends again.

Throughout our married life, my wife and I have used techniques that have helped us to survive the most difficult of times. I would like to share these with you. I have found in talking to many couples over the years that most don't have the basic tools to survive the many storms that can befall a couple during their married life. Without tools, even the strongest of marriages can hit the rocks with devastating results.

In the following pages, you will see examples of three marriages. They are from three different eras and fraught with different challenges. Along with the discussion of these three marriages, there are other equally important topics that will be discussed such as: words we say to each other, physician marriages, and insight into exactly why people marry. After each chapter, you will be given questions to allow you to engage in meaningful and thoughtful exercises and discussions with your significant other.

This book has been a labor of love to both research and to write. I have spent my life endeavoring to positively impact the lives of people in the practice of medicine. Now, I want to make an equally powerful and lingering impact on the lives of people through marriage and engaged couple coaching.

I am not a marriage therapist though I have counseled numerous people individually, as well as couples in my family practice. I am happy to see favorable outcomes in the lives of many people who I have touched.

What I am is a marriage coach as well as an engaged couples' coach with over 20 years' experience. I have done so through retreats as well as private sessions with individuals and couples who have sought me out for advice as a physician as well as a happily and successfully married man for over 27 years. Many people are aware of the adversities I have had to endure personally, as well as those Vanessa and I have endured as a couple.

A marriage counselor is someone who deals with the past in a relationship and who has had specific psychological training in helping marital couples. Counseling is for couples who need more specialized help to address past hurts, mental health issues, or other behaviors that are beyond coaching. It often focuses on understanding the past to create health in the present. Some couples need therapy, some do better with coaching. Therapy is a much more formal atmosphere than coaching and can be very intimidating for some couples.

A marriage coach deals with the future and how we can attain that future. Coaching creates a partnership between the coach and the couples. Couples are often knowledgeable to some extent about their relationship in a coaching setting, and ultimately have some answers to what they're looking for. They just need guidance and an unbiased coach to get there. A marriage coach determines what goals the couples have for the future and then helps them achieve them. Coaches are mirrors that reflect to a couple what they are seeing. They are an unbiased third party. You may ask, can a coach help with all marital problems? If a problem is not determined to be coachable or if there is an issue that the couple cannot resolve, the couple should be and will be referred to a mental health professional for counseling.

Without the love of my God, my children, and my best friend in life, this book would not be possible.

Dr. Jeep and his wife, Vanessa

PROLOGUE

This book would not have been possible without the help and insight of a man who helped inspire me to write it, Dr. Jarret Patton, MD.

Dr. Patton is a man amongst men whose goal in life has always been to be there for his fellow man. He has been there for me. The heart of this child of God is undeniable, and he has been the wind beneath my wings.

I would also like to thank my children: Chelsey, Chantal, and Phillip, all of whom make me proud to be their father every day. They are the product of a loving marriage and are three kind and decent people. They reflect the best of their mother and father.

I would be remiss if I did not mention my best friend and true soulmate in life, my wife, Vanessa. Honey, you are the peace amidst the storm; you are the rock upon which our marriage has been built. You have brought me unimaginable joy and I love you.

Finally, and most importantly, I give thanks to my God who has always been with me and has inspired me while writing. The institution of marriage starts and ends with Him. He brings us together so the two shall become one. In becoming one, we better ourselves and those around us in loving commitment. Love isn't truly love until you also give it away to others.

His part in my life can best be described in the poem "Footprints." In it, a man (at the end of his life) asks God where he has been during the rocky times. He says to God, "I saw your footprints next to mine during my life but when I was suffering the most, your footprints were gone." God answered him and said, "My precious, precious child, it is during those times that I carried you" (1).

Of that I believe, there is no doubt.

CHAPTER I
WHY MARRY?

The primary word that comes to mind when asking "why marry" is commitment.

Publicly declaring your love in front of friends and family in a formal ceremony makes your coupleness feel meaningful in a way that simply living together does not.

A marriage contract puts a protective shell around your relationship that helps keep your bond strong when there are bumps in the road. It gives couples the sense of security that they'll stay together no matter what.

Being married causes you to feel and act like a team. Married couples experience a transformation. You start to work together to achieve the best outcomes for the both of you as opposed to acting on your own to get things that each of you want. Essentially, you take on one another's dreams and form a new set of mutual goals.

It's common for married couples to settle into a sense of security in marriage. Because marriage is the ultimate level of commitment that our society recognizes, it signifies that you've reached the hope and dream of a lifelong satisfying and loving relationship.

The purpose of marriage is to spiritually, emotionally, and physically unite a man and a woman together as husband and wife. It is one of the most important commitments two people can make during their lifetimes.

The main reason to get married is the same reason it's important to do virtually every good thing in life: to avoid being too into yourself—being "you" centered instead of "we" centered. Being you centered is the enemy of commitment. If you are the center of your own life, people will eventually figure that out. It means you've never found anything outside of yourself more important to you than yourself. It means you DON'T KNOW how to love or you are afraid.

The choice everyone has to make regarding their life is to either spend it alone or to spend it with someone else. Marriage not only fosters love, it teaches love. In marriage, we have to love permanently, consciously, and purposefully every day, no matter what. Marriage is hard to create; however, it is through this process that we finally connect everything that comprises our best hopes and dreams.

According to Gottman, "When people really love and they make a commitment, they become enormously vulnerable and enormously powerful because they care so much and it connects them to the world in a huge way. All of these benefits are established by commitment. The commitment is like falling over backwards, and it translates into making you a concerned human being.

Somebody who is involved in the community of mankind" (2).

Marriage eliminates or should eliminate loneliness. Through challenges, individually and together, couples mature. Children are blessings of the marital bond and they get a front row seat to see and experience the lasting benefits of a strong family. Marriage contributes to society because it serves as a model to show the world the way women and men live interdependently in commitment for life. The goal is to be the best and to seek the best for each other along the marital journey. A journey filled with greater happiness and increased intimacy as you live out your lives together. Additionally, the marital union provides the best conditions for raising children, namely the stable, loving relationship of a mother and a father present in a committed marriage. Children are socialized to become productive members of society who replace those who die. In today's society, which consists mainly of impersonal secondary relationships, living in a mutually emotional and supportive environment is particularly important.

Marriage has several health benefits: longer life, fewer heart attacks and strokes, and less depression (3).

Children in healthy, loving homes with married biological parents can learn to navigate relationships and aim to have a successful marriage of their own. Research suggests that intact marriages serve as a stable household with fewer arrests than broken family homes (3).

When people believe in and achieve healthy and happy marriages, it stands to reason that marriage is important to society because both men and women stand to live longer when they're in healthy marriages. Husbands and wives build wealth together more easily. Children who grow up in stable homes typically achieve more. Women in healthy, loving marital relationships are less likely to be involved in domestic violence. A good marriage teaches children about love, sacrifice, and selflessness. Thus, developing more emotionally aware and behaviorally stable individuals who will care for others, not to mention, teach them what they should expect from their future partners (3). The positive attributes of a good marriage are plentiful.

Today's motto, "If it feels good, do it," highlights a view of human beings as animals. It perpetuates the belief that people should do what pleases them at the moment without a thought to the broader, long-term consequences of their actions (3).

Marriage is under assault in the public arena. The right to privacy rulings by activist judges is not about the common good but about "me." The reason marriages are important is that they affirm what the Founding Fathers understood: that the purpose of this country is to use our freedoms for the promotion of the common good (3).

Society is failing to affirm the vital institution of marriage which is under assault with high rates of divorce and out of wedlock births (3).

Within the context of marriage, 44 percent of children are less likely to be physically abused, 47 percent are less likely to suffer physical neglect, 43 percent are less likely to suffer emotional neglect, and 55 percent are less likely to suffer from some form of child abuse (3).

Research shows that married women have 30 percent better health, are less likely to suffer chronic disabilities or chronic health, and their mortality rates are one third that of single women. Also, they are far less likely to suffer from domestic violence (3).

Men are more likely to be involved in the community in service organizations. Mortality rates are 30 percent less than unmarried men. Men are less likely to commit suicide and they are generally healthier than single men (3).

Marriage is the training ground for the adult world. Children learn to become citizens and they learn about relationships in society. They learn how to act and how to be responsible.

The state of marriage and family is a good indicator of the state of our society. Marriage helps people to develop a virtue in their lives.

Many couple's enter marriage without the tools to get married. The vows are taken as a ritual without truly understanding or caring about what they actually mean. Many couples do not know how to handle the stressors that life brings. They know how to handle the good times but not the bad times.

Many churches don't offer programs that provide couples with the tools to weather marital storms. Therefore, couples basically are unprepared. If programs are offered, they are often understaffed and are not made mandatory. The programs are only as good as the effort and the knowledge that the couples who present them have. Marriage is not treasured and valued like it once was. So often, it is looked upon as a disposable institution, to be thrown away with ease instead of working hard for it to succeed as it was intended. There is an entire legal industry that continues to swell due to the eagerness to throw away marriage. The statistics are well-known. More than 50 percent of marriages end in divorce. The marriage rate itself is declining. It is an American tragedy of enormous proportions. The fact that we live in an increasingly secular society also shows that there is no religion in the marital house. The marriage is not based on or dedicated to religious principles. In order for marriage to both survive and thrive, there must be religious principles and values at the core of relationships.

The Dalai Lama has said that too many people in the West have given up on marriage. They don't, according to him, understand that it is about developing a mutual admiration of someone, and a deep respect and trust and awareness of another humans' needs. He says that the new easy come, easy go relationships give couples more freedom but less contentment (4).

Getting married is a public demonstration of love and lifelong commitment between two people. Christians believe that marriage is a beautiful symbol of God's love for his bride, the church. In the binding partnership of marriage is a powerful symbol of this relationship. When at it's best, marriage can show us a glimpse of the faithful enduring love which God has toward his people (5).

The Church of Jesus Christ of Latter-day Saints believes marriage is a covenant between a man and a woman and God. The belief in repentance, forgiveness, integrity, and love provides the remedy for conflict in marriage (6).

The Roman Catholic Church teaches that God Himself is the author of the sacred institution of marriage, which is His way of showing love for those He created. Man and woman, although created differently from each other, complement each other. The complementarity draws them together in a mutual and loving union (7).

The above are but a few examples. Every major religion has vital opinions about marriage with principles to follow. If religion does not exist and if God is not present, there are no principles to follow and the marriage suffers. Couples can use the strength of their faith to get them through the rough patches in life.

I believe marriage is between a man and a women; however, I do not want to alienate same-sex or non-monogamous couples who could be helped by my book. My faith tells me not to judge, and I believe that the principles in this book can help all relationships.

CHAPTER I QUESTIONS

1) Why did you get married?

_____

_____

_____

_____

2) Do you agree with the stated reasons as to why people get married? If so, why? If not, why not?

_____

_____

_____

_____

3) Do you agree that the institution of marriage is in trouble? If so, why? If not, why not?

_____

_____

_____

_____

4) Do you agree that children raised in a loving, stable, and married family atmosphere is good for society? If so, why? If not, why not?

_____

_____

_____

_____

5) As someone who is married, do you see the health benefits of being married? If so, what health benefits have you noticed?

_____

_____

_____

_____

6) Do you agree that religion is a central part of a good marital union? If so, why? If not, why not?

_____

_____

_____

_____

7) Are you happy that you decided to marry? If so, why?
If not, why not?

_____

_____

_____

_____

CHAPTER 2
WORDS

Words are powerful things!

St. James said, "How great a forest is set ablaze by such a small fire! The tongue is a fire, a world of unrighteousness" (8).

Words can destroy relationships, instill fear, create limitations, and engender strife. Words can also heal, give birth to faith in vision, and more importantly be used to forgive and love.

Each of us will either be a master of our own words or be mastered by them. The words we release into our lives and into the lives of others can carry love, and faith, or lead to the confusion and destruction of people.

When we speak, let us learn to consider our words carefully. Are they coming from a good place or a bad one? Are we reacting from emotion or pausing to truly realize what we are saying and the consequences of what we are saying? Our words are like a superpower. Use them for good and not evil, to build and not to destroy, and to credit not discredit.

According to Webster, a word is "A sound or a combination of sounds, or a representation in writing or printing, that symbolizes and communicates a meaning and may consist of a single theme or a combination of themes" (9).

"It is something said, an utterance, remark or comment. For example, 'Not another word!' It is a command or direction; an order, an assurance or a promise, sworn intention, a verbal sign, password or a watchword" (9).

Our words carry enormous weight. More weight than we sometimes think. They often impact people for decades, providing either the courage to press on or more reasons to give up. As a kid in a new school, a student came up to me and said, "Man, are your eyes crossed!" I was mortified. I didn't know what to say. I wanted to cry but I managed a little laugh, like it didn't really bother me. But it did. Every day from that point forward, I would look at myself in the mirror and all I could see were those crossed eyes. I studied them from every angle but kept coming back to the point that I was horrible looking. Thankfully, I eventually grew out of it. It just goes to show how powerful words can be. A careless word can shape or misshape someone's reality of themselves for years to come.

I try to live by the following examples of wisdom every day to make a more positive influence using my words. There are three characteristics of positive speech:

1) Positive speech can build people up. That applies to everyone that we encounter including stressed out family members. Words have the potential to build them up or

tear them down. The power is mostly in our words. It takes more than good thoughts and deeds to build people up. The real creative potential for change lies in the words we use. Positive words develop the people around us.

2) Positive words are timely. The correct words at the wrong time can be just as damaging as the wrong words. When someone experiences a major setback or a disappointment for example, we need to be careful not to dismiss their pain or frustration. It is usually a bad idea to lecture them about what they could or should have done differently. Words left unsaid can be hurtful. I once worked for a woman who literally never acknowledged, affirmed, or praised my performance. She only acknowledged my mistakes. Any encouraging words would've cost her nothing and would have meant the world to me, but she didn't do it.

3) Positive words provide a benefit. Relationships take more than merely being generous or accommodating, though these are both important. The words we say do something active and positive in the lives of others. Our words can either empower people and encourage them or diminish them and make them want to quit. Words can be used to build or destroy. They are either life-giving or life-taking. For example, I remember going through a bad time at one point. I called my dad and his words provided encouragement. They were just what I needed: reassuring, encouraging, and confidence building. His words were like manna from Heaven. They gave

me the energy to hang in there and keep fighting. They gave me the grace I needed to do the right thing for my family and for my future.

Every day, we are shaping reality for someone by the words we use. Do you know people who fly off the handle without stopping to think about the consequences of what they're saying? Someone who just reacts to something someone else said or starts attacking that person with cruel accusations? I have to honestly say I have been guilty of this and in many situations I have paid for it. However, I have learned from my behavior. The damage caused by your words could be profound and forever sever relationships. You've probably observed this in others many times. Whether it's at work, with friends, or in some type of social situation, many people speak their minds before thinking. I have cringed when this happens because I know people are going to get hurt. Later on, people will be sorry for what they said but the damage is done.

Within the words we speak is an emotional potency. Each word can have a colossal impact. A word may initially seem inconsequential but never think of words as inconsequential. They can motivate or discourage. Words influence others and build relationships, or they can tear down relationships. Simply put, language holds a massive power to manifest good or bad change.

Speak every word you say in life as though it was your last. "If you can't say something nice, don't say nothing at all," as Thumper's mother said (10). Benjamin Franklin said, "Remember not only to say the right thing in the right place, but far more difficult still, is to leave unsaid the wrong thing at a tempting moment" (11).

Choose the words that you speak very carefully because they have the potential to accomplish nearly anything or destroy everything. Just one negative comment can make a day or potentially ruin many successive days, weeks, or even longer. A few negative comments might even ruin a person's life. One positive and encouraging word can make more of a difference in an individual's life than you could ever know. We tend to overlook the small things in life. The way we speak and our attitude, tone, and volume reflects the person we are. It impacts everything around us. It can greatly contribute to your success or failure in your personal life. Again, I know this firsthand. Next time think before you speak and it will make a difference. Yet, no matter how meticulously you plan your words, you can never control how your message is received. Knowing what is within your power and preparing in advance will help to maximize communication.

Each conversation you leave with regrets shares a common denominator––you didn't think before you spoke. Most of us are at our best when we have ample time to process our thoughts before sharing them. Put yourself in the other person's shoes when forming your approach. A point brought up with logic and confidence is less likely to be met with hostility. The key is to approach each conversation with an open mind. Emotions often trump logic. Don't underestimate the influence that emotions can play in how a message is received. Many disagreements between people occur due to differences in their understanding of the meaning of words. When communicating through words, we often think about ourselves. Words coming from a good place make life brighter. If a positive word was powerful in a conversation, then we will long have a good feeling of its value to us.

The power of the spoken word has energy and the ability to heal, hinder, hurt, harm, humiliate, and humble. According to Yehuda Berg, "We must discipline ourselves to speak in a way that conveys respect, gentleness, and humility. One of the clearest signs of a moral life is right speech" (12).

Many of us are driven to speak to any passing feeling, thought, or impression we have. We randomly dump the contents of our mind on others while we speak without regard to the significance of what we are saying. We don't think before we speak. When we speak on trivial matters, such as gossiping about others, our attention is wasted on trivialities. When we speak, we should speak with understanding in a way to bring about peace and compassion in our character. We should always be truthful and avoid exaggerations when we are speaking. Also, we shouldn't use double standards when addressing people or use our words to manipulate others. Most importantly, we should not use words to insult or belittle anyone.

When we need to talk candidly with another person about something that is difficult, we must focus on what is being said and purposely pay keen attention. During the conversation, we must listen patiently, speak tactfully, and tell the truth as we understand it.

In closing, we need to remember and understand the quote, "Before you speak, THINK. For example, use The THINK Technique:

T- Is it thoughtful?

H- Is it honest?

I- Is it intelligent?

N- Is it necessary?

K- Is it kind?" (13)

CHAPTER 2 QUESTIONS

1) What was your overall impression of this chapter?

_____

_____

_____

_____

2) Have you come to understand the importance of words in every day communication with others? With your spouse?

_____

_____

_____

_____

3) Do you understand the quote, "Before you speak, THINK." How important is it in the context of communicating with your spouse? (13).

_____

_____

_____

_____

4) Do you understand the quote, "Don't talk unless you can improve the silence," by Jorge Luis Borges? (14) If so, how does it pertain to marriage communication?

_____

_____

_____

_____

CHAPTER 3
THE MARRIAGE OF DELORES AND PHILLIP: IN SICKNESS AND IN HEALTH

Delores and Phillip were married in 1931. From the very start, the marriage was fraught with life's difficulties. Delores married a first-generation immigrant from Macedonia who through hard work and dedication achieved admission to a very prestigious medical school. He came from humble beginnings and wanted to practice in an underserved area. And there was no more underserved of an area than a coal mining town in southern West Virginia. This was back in the days when the coal company was king. The coal company owned the town where Phillip lived and worked. All accessories were bought and paid for at the company store. There was no cash exchanged for goods. Everything was bought with company scrip. Coal scrip is tokens or paper with a monetary value issued to workers as an advance on wages by the coal company or its designated representative. As such, coal scrip could only be used at the specific locality or coal town of the company named. It was the currency that was used amongst the coal mine and the miners in exchange for goods and services in that locality. Delores and Phillip lived better than those that he served, but not a whole lot better. Workers were paid little and could barely keep up with essentials like food, water, and clothing. Phillip would often take no scrip from his patients, and on many occasions actually would give them scrip as a donation. He knew they were in such incredible need. He would often barter for his services with patients; for example, accepting a bushel of corn, a chicken, or a chore to fix something at his home. This was the kind of man he was. This is the man Delores fell in love with. She knew what she was getting into regarding the demands of his profession. She knew her life could be better financially and materially by marring a physician. Marrying him came with the cost of long nights on call, him being at work most of the day, and work that he inevitably brought home with him. However, that's not why she married him. She married him because of his kind, decent, and compassionate traits. Because of his kindness, compassion, and sympathy for the people he served, it was impossible for him not to dwell on their problems as well. Dwelling on their problems meant that at times when he was at home, he was not truly present for her.

Delores also went into her marriage knowing that Phillip had a medical problem that began in childhood and would get progressively worse with time. He contracted rheumatic fever at a time when treatment for the problem was nearly non-existent. Rheumatic fever is caused by a bacterial infection that if not successfully treated can result in devastating injury to the heart as well as to the joints. Unfortunately, he became afflicted with injuries to both. The bacteria can destroy heart valves which causes progressive deterioration of the function of the heart. Although she eventually became a nurse, Delores didn't fully understand the implications of Phillip's medical problem.

When living in southern West Virginia, Phillip often worked such long hours that the strain would cause him to become exhausted. Delores would nurse him back to health as well as keep the house together. Delores and Phillip had two young sons, John and Michael, and one can only imagine the stress she was dealing with. She took her vows seriously as most couples did back then. The vows say: "In sickness and in health." As time went on, there was plenty of sickness and very little health. Notice in the vows that there is a description of opposites-- in sickness and in health. These situations depict what can be good and enjoyable, but what can also try even the strongest of unions.

As time went by, Phillip's health grew worse. The family was forced to move to northern West Virginia, back to where Delores was originally from. Delores had much more help with matters of the household due to having family around her. Phillip, due to the progressive worsening of his heart condition, became less and less able to work and spent more and more time convalescing. Since northern West Virginia is a temperate climate (there are four seasons in that area), some convalescing had to take place in a warmer climate. Due to the kindness of others, Delores and Phillip were able to go to Florida often for months at a time. The children frequently went to stay with relatives so they were regularly uprooted (sometimes for months on end) and had to attend different schools, make new friends, and leave old ones behind. The cycle would repeat itself, sometimes several times a year. It caused chaos in the family. The children were left feeling abandoned and bitter as their father's health deteriorated. Delores persisted although leaving her kids was gut-wrenching and many times personally devastating. She did what was necessary for her husband.

In his letter to the Thessalonians about persistence, St. Paul says in 2 Thessalonians 3:13-15, "But yeah, brethren, be not weary in well doing" (15). Delores certainly was an example of that. Oftentimes, if you don't put your relationship first, your marriage will not survive.
Communication with your children is very important. They have to know that mommy and daddy working on their marriage has to happen first so that mommy and daddy can be good for them in the long run. Much like we're told when traveling in an airplane to put our oxygen masks on first so that we can fully, without compromise,

assist a child, this should also be true in a marriage with children. Couples need couple-time to stay connected, deepen their love, and allow friendship and sexual intimacy to blossom. Lack of communication between couples can cause irreparable damage to family dynamics for years to come, destroying trust and causing bitterness. Instead of growing in love and intimacy together, couples can drift apart. Dealing with life's twists and turns together as they arise while you are raising your family is much easier than having to deal with resentment and disillusionment later in your marriage. In a subsequent chapter, this topic will be discussed more fully.

With time, Phillip became weaker and unable to work. Available treatments, which were limited, became ineffective and he eventually succumbed to his disease. He died at the age of 40.

Delores was devastated and grief stricken, but she knew she had to gather herself together and move on for her children. She would never remarry, feeling that no one could ever measure up to her one true love. This was not unusual for her generation which Tom Brokaw called "The Greatest Generation."

CHAPTER 3 QUESTIONS

1) What were the positive aspects of Delores' character and behavior? Did you learn anything positive from her?

_____

_____

_____

_____

2) What were the negative aspects of Delores' character and behavior? Did you learn anything negative from her?

_____

_____

_____

_____

3) What were the positive aspects of Phillip's character and behavior? Did you learn anything positive from him?

_____

_____

_____

_____

4) What were the negative aspects of Phillip's character and behavior? Did you learn anything negative from him?

_____

_____

_____

_____

5) Are any of the positive or negative aspects of Delores' character or behavior reflective of similar behavior or character traits in your own marriage or life?

_____

_____

_____

_____

6) Are any of the positive or negative aspects of Phillip's character or behavior reflective of similar behavior or character traits in your own marriage or life?

_____

_____

_____

_____

7) What is your overall impression of Delores and Phillip's marriage? Were they lifegiving to each other?

_____

_____

_____

_____

CHAPTER 4
JOHN'S BEGINNINGS

John was about nine years of age at the time of his father's death. He was now a part of a single parent household, not by divorce but by death which is often more devastating. For the majority of John's formative years, he was without a father figure in his life and essentially had been for most of his early years due to his father having been absent because of work and health issues. Coaches, uncles, grandfathers, and mentors can help fill the gap, but no one can replace a father. Without a male role model, one's outlook on marriage and other important building blocks in life are often, understandably, compromised. John was essentially raised by his mother. Because he was the oldest, John was forced at a young age to be the father in the family. He had to be the example not only for his brother and his sister but for his mother. He had to work for everything he got. He had a paper route. Later on, during his teenage years, he worked in the steel mills during the summer. The money he made went to his mother. Working helped build responsibility, but giving all of his earnings to his mother led to anger and resentment that would show its ugly head once John got married. John loved to play sports so he played several, and he was very good at everything he played. But, he could only play by making good grades and he had to be able to work at the same time. He accomplished those things and it fostered the growth of his self-esteem. Self-esteem is a great thing, but too much of it can lead to arrogance and an overinflated ego. Again, those are traits that would haunt him later once he got married.

As he grew older, he began to resent being told what to do by his mother, by his elders, or by anyone else. Since he worked for what he earned, his attitude was that the money was his and he would share it if and how he saw fit. What he did in his life mattered most and what anyone else did mattered maybe a little, but he was the king in his relationships. He resented women and being told what to do by them. Even though he was raised by a woman, his mother, he grew up in a time when women were considered secondary and subservient to men. Women were to be seen and not heard, and to have babies and raise children. However, raising children was not considered to be real work. At least that was what John thought. After high school, due to his strong work ethic, John earned a scholarship to play basketball in college. This ended up being a disaster. According to him, the coach was a man of large ego and was anything but fair. John continued to work hard to try and earn a starting spot on the team but according to him nothing was good enough for the coach. The coach was well-known and had a statue out-side of the gym in his likeness. Every time John passed by that statue, he would spit on it. He endured the tension between himself and the coach for two years but decided that he could put up with it no longer and quit the team. Since he had no money to go to college and now no schol-arship, he had to drop out. This was at a time when the military draft was still in existence. Men were able to be excluded if they were in college. But, as soon as they left college, they became eligible for the draft. Indeed, John was drafted into the Army. He was required to spend two years in the service—one year in the United States and one year at a base in another company.

His experience in college seeded his resentment for the world and his lot in life. The fact, in his mind, was that he worked hard but there was always someone above him telling him what to do. That infuriated him. The worst place he could go was to the Army. It didn't matter that he was performing a service to his country and that it was altruistic and honorable; he was not going to be told what to do by someone who was inferior to him. He was going to have to listen, like it or not, to someone who he felt was less intelligent than him. His disgust at being told what to do boiled over and he could not wait to be out and on his own and in charge of his own life. Nobody would ever again tell him what to do. Even if they were able to, he wouldn't listen. Even if it was proven to be in his best interest, he wouldn't do it unless it suited him.

When John was in the Army, he sent most of his money home to his mother. The money helped her and his siblings who were still home. It was also in the Army, however, that he got a taste of gambling. He would play cards for money and like most people who love gambling, he always embellished his winnings and downplayed his losses. Also like many gamblers, he always thought he could win back what he lost by playing another game. This was a habit John continued for years to come.

When he was discharged from the service, he wanted to go back to school. He would only be able to do so by working as well as qualifying for the GI Bill. Going to college and working went well for him, but he would never overcome the hang-up of having conflicts with people telling him what to do.

He eventually reconnected with a woman named Elaine that he had dated in high school. They became very close. She lived in the town where he went to college and he had originally met her during a basketball tournament when they were both in high school. She thought he was cute and was extremely attracted to him because he was a very good athlete especially in basketball, though he played other sports. She was a cheerleader, and a very attractive one at that. Nothing happened in high school because she was three years younger than him.

Now, he was older and so was she and it seemed like a good time to start up a romance. He was working hard at his dream of becoming a doctor. She was living at home with her parents but also working. When he was not in school, he was working at a very difficult job at night while also trying to study. She would dutifully wait for him to leave work so they could spend time together before he went to class. As months passed, they became closer and closer.

Elaine was an only child of two very doting parents who thought the sun rose and set on their daughter. Her father was very protective of her and dutifully inspected every man that came to the house. John was indifferent. In his heart, he resented being scrutinized by his future father-in-law and didn't feel that he should ever be treated with such disdain or skepticism. Her father was just another person who was giving him a hard time and telling him what to do. That just made John more self-centered. He was determined to be his own man and to do things his way regardless of how others felt.

He continued to work very hard in and out of school. He belonged to a fraternity which gave him a sense of belonging. He was around people who didn't tell him what to do, people he could be himself with and who had similar interests and attitudes about women.

John eventually graduated with a science degree and applied to medical school. He didn't get in the first time he applied which was another blow given to him by someone else telling him what to do. However, perseverance was and still is a great quality of his which has taken him far professionally.

CHAPTER 4 QUESTIONS

1) What are some of the positive aspects of John's character and behavior during his early life that you may have learned from? If you learned lessons, what did you learn?

_____

_____

_____

_____

2) What are some of the negative aspects of John's character and behavior during his early life that you may have learned from? If you learned lessons, what did you learn?

_____

_____

_____

_____

3) Can you see how his premarital attitudes developed? If so, how?

_____

_____

_____

_____

4) Can you think of couples who kept aspects of their true selves a secret during the courtship prior to their marriage? In what ways have you kept your true self a secret during courtship? What do you fear?

_____

_____

_____

_____

CHAPTER 5
THE MARRIAGE OF JOHN AND ELAINE: PROBLEMS FROM THE START

After graduation, John married his girlfriend Elaine. They had a wonderful and beautiful wedding, but John's relationship with Elaine's father remained rocky. It eventually improved, especially when the grandchildren came along.

Fast forward five years. John has finished medical school and moved his family back to his hometown in northern West Virginia. He and Elaine now have three kids, but they are living with John's mother because there is not enough money to buy a house. Fortunately, his mother has enough bedrooms for herself, John and Elaine, and the three kids. It was a very hard pill to swallow for John to not be able to afford a house on his own. Again, he had to listen to other people and live under someone else's roof. He was working in a local hospital doing his internship and making very little money. Working hard and putting in the hours was never an issue for John; however, it made him more selfish with the money he was making. He thought, *This is my money!* No one worked harder for it than he did. He would share it as he saw fit, but it was never before his own needs and desires were met. He was selfish and dictatorial with his money when it came to sharing it with his mother, wife, and children. Whether people knew it or not, giving or sharing what he had was never completely out of the goodness of John's heart. There would always be a price to pay at some point for those he shared his money with.

One year later, John bought a new house for himself and his family and started his own practice. The family now consisted of four children, three boys and one girl. He wanted three boys and two girls, and that was going to happen regardless of what his wife wanted. He was going to have what he wanted because it was what he wanted, and that's what mattered most.

John continued to work and build his medical practice. Elaine took care of the kids which was no easy task. Between the oldest and the youngest, there was a span of five years. There were times when three of the four children were in diapers. John felt that it was Elaine's duty to take care of the kids without his help because that was her job. If he took part in it, it was if and when he had time. He greatly devalued the work Elaine did and discounted what it took not only to raise children, but to raise them right. In fact, he didn't put Elaine's work with the children on a par with his work as a doctor. He didn't think it was nearly as important. After all, he was the one who was making the money. He was the breadwinner. She was bringing in no money. Since she was bringing in no money, she really had no say, in his opinion. He looked at cleaning the house and cooking dinner much the same way. They were difficult jobs, but he didn't equate her work with being as valuable as his. Despite the fact that cooking his dinner and cleaning the house made doing his job easier and more productive, her work still wasn't as important as his.

Seeds sown in his early life began to be replanted in his marriage. John continued to gamble. He would gamble with money that he didn't have. If he was losing, it didn't matter. In his mind, he would always be able to win it back. But the more he tried to do that, the more he lost. It didn't matter if the money from the disposable income was gone. It didn't matter if part of their disposable income was Elaine's. After all, this was HIS money and he would use it when he wanted to. If continuing to gamble meant dipping into expense money for bills, food, and clothing, it didn't matter. He would either win it back or he would find a way to get the money. After all, he was a doctor now and he thought his status could get him what he needed. He reasoned, "I can always get money from the bank. I'm good for it and they know that." If payments from the bank came due, then he always had his friends to help him out if need be.

Funny thing about his friends, John always bragged about how good they were. He had many of them. After all, John was a nice enough guy. They would do things for him and he would do things for them. However, whatever he did was for a price. He had no shame about going to a friend and asking them for money. He exhibited that same lack of shame later in life when he repeatedly asked to borrow money from his kids. It seemed like his friends were always there for him when he asked for money even if lending it to him hurt them financially. John was a charmer and he was always good at manipulating people. He would do it to anyone to get what he wanted.

Staying out and gambling until all hours of the night was something John thought he richly deserved. It didn't matter that he wasn't spending necessary time with his kids. He was spending time doing what he thought he needed to do and what he felt he deserved. He felt like he was a king and kings did what they wanted regardless of the opinion of others "below" them. That was an attitude that continued to fester for years and it would cause nothing but heartache.

John had made many friends throughout his lifetime. Making friends helped his self-esteem. Unfortunately, his friendships were put at a premium above the interests of his family. He was giving time to his friends that sorely needed to be put into his relationship with his wife and children.

Elaine had given up whatever interest she had in herself and focused her attention on John and their four children. She desperately wanted to have a family and be a good wife, but John made that extremely difficult to do because he was scarcely at home. And when he was at home, he didn't make a lot of time for their marriage or for what she wanted to do. He really didn't spend a lot of time with the children either. But John was raised with good values and he imparted them into his children. He disciplined them when necessary, most of the time with the right mixture of physical and psychological discipline. For example, his discipline consisted of talks of his disappointment with the children, withholding privileges and allowances, etc. However, sometimes he disciplined them in anger, using too much physical discipline as well as hurtful words and phrases like, "Are you that stupid?" or "You can't be that dumb." Discipline used incorrectly can have a long-lasting and devastating effect on a child or adolescent.

Elaine wasn't without her faults. Physical discipline was not her forte, screaming was. If screaming didn't work, then the dreaded, "Wait until your father gets home!" was used. John and Elaine were never on the same page regarding discipline, but they were on the same page regarding their desire to raise decent, respectful, and productive members of society. To get back at John, Elaine would spend money. Money they didn't have. She would bounce checks. John took care of the finances and he was worse than she was. This was a match made in financial hell.

When John would stay out late, Elaine would get angry. Often, he would come home after being out all night without even the respect of a phone call. Many times, he would come home just to leave again to go to work for the day. He would then come home exhausted, say very little to anyone, and fall asleep in his chair. Sleep was often preceded by a number of cocktails. For years, John had an issue with alcohol both at home and when he and Elaine would go out. Bourbon and Coke or Vodka Stingers were his drinks of choice when they went out. He would drink excessively and the drinks would give him a false sense of power and invincibility. He was narcissistic and would unnecessarily brag about himself to the point of being unseemly. If his friends were disgusted by his behavior, they would never say so. Then again, why would they? Many of them were carbon copies of him. Elaine would often remain silent or when she did speak up it would cause a fight in the car on the way home.

This unhealthy behavior went on for years. Elaine would get angry, and it would cause a loud and heated discussion with the kids often within hearing distance. John's first-born son would frequently hear what was going on and it would frighten him as well as his younger siblings. What would happen after the argument was predictable. There would be a period of tension and then there would be an apology, mostly by Elaine because John was too arrogant to admit any wrongdoing. Then, there would be a honeymoon period. John would drink less, go out less, and stay home more. But that wouldn't last long because of John's conceit and arrogance. As was typical, he would say to himself, *Why should I listen to what she says? I am the breadwinner, and I'm the one who does most of the work. I don't care what she says! I can and will do whatever, whenever I want, for as long as I want!* So, the cycle continued for years and their relationship progressively deteriorated.

John had little respect for women. The lack of respect began early on in his life when his mother was the sole parent but most importantly the disciplinarian. Women to him had their place but were never equal to men and never should have authority over men. They were to stay home, "barefoot and pregnant." They were not to work. Staying home and taking care of the kids was their job. They were to be subservient to men and be there for their every want and need. Whatever money was given to his family was at his discretion. Sex was to be at his beck and call. And whether orgasm happened or his wife was pleasured was of little concern to him.

Elaine and John argued incessantly even before they were married. The more they argued, the less respect he had for her and vice versa. How could she respect a man who treated her the way he did? How could she show affection to a man who gave her so little time and such little respect? His idea of affection was sex and his orgasm. He had never learned real affection because early in his life affection was limited. The more Elaine pulled away, the more John resented her. John developed a wandering eye.

As a doctor, he had ample opportunity and many excuses for being out late or even out all night for that matter. He would think, *She's not meeting my needs. She's not respecting me!* Since Elaine wasn't doing those things, he rationalized that adultery was not something that was a problem. She deserved it. His needs had to be met and if they weren't, he had every right to find a woman that would give him what he deserved. He would stay in the marriage because he felt responsible for the children. *Elaine made her bed so she can lay in it,* he thought. If she had sexual needs, he would be there to satisfy them, but he would continue his affair because the other woman was giving him what he needed.

Those women gave John what he needed most––his ego built up. They would build up his self-esteem. They were sycophants telling him what a great person he was, what a great father he was, and what a great doctor he was. He gave them status and that massaged their egos. John would tire of those women eventually, but the damage was already done to his marriage with Elaine. As their marriage progressed, their relationship deteriorated even more.

It was John's decision to have five children. With the five children came increasing responsibilities. Taking care of five children was not inexpensive and that was something that John came to resent. The first house he bought was a good starter house in a nice neighborhood. It was the type of neighborhood with many kids, many young families, and a close-knit community. It was the type of neighborhood where you could always leave your door open and friends were plentiful. John, however, wanted more. He was always planning for more and had money earmarked for what he wanted to do with it before he had it. Besides being devious with affairs, John would let nothing stand in the way of what he wanted even if it meant bending the rules. He was always determined to have the best of everything. He rationalized that he went long enough through childhood, adolescence, and early adulthood not having what he wanted, so nothing would stand in the way of having the best of what he wanted now.

When John's dream house came on the market, it was enormous, but outdated and in desperate need of repair. John told Elaine that he wanted to buy the house. She was satisfied with where the family was living. She had many friends and didn't want to move. The house needed more money to be updated than what they could afford. Elaine refused to sign the loan for the house. So, what did John do? He forged her signature. She was furious but the deed was done.

Eventually, Elaine grew to like and enjoy the house especially decorating it. She had a flair for being artistic and it showed. She also had a bit of expensive taste. So, when the bills came in, it infuriated John which as usual caused arguments. Life continued. The kids grew and were well educated from going to private schools which John resented. He would remind them later in life about his sacrifice in letting them go there.

Nothing was going to change though regarding expenses. His gambling, his trips, and his women would still all be paid for as well as family expenses. He would just let the bills pile up. Finally, the financial neglect came to a head. It became clear that John could no longer afford to keep the house and maintain his otherwise expensive lifestyle as well as the mountains of bills and loans that needed to be paid. Elaine had come to like the house. She had put much time and effort into it. Due to her near professional decorating touch, the antiquated house was turned into a truly artistic piece of real estate worthy of listings in magazines such as *Southern Living* and *Architectural Digest*. Knowing what it had been, people who passed by were astonished to see what it had become.

Elaine was devastated. The thought that she was going to have to move was both mind-numbing and physically exhausting. As usual, this was John's decision and she had very little if any say in the matter. Because he handled the finances and kept things from her completely, Elaine had no idea how bad off they truly were financially. As she found out, even with selling the house, whatever money they would make would go to pay debts that she had no idea were owed. John's attitude about money would continually be his undoing and caused undesirable personal and professional consequences because he was forced to declare bankruptcy.

Bankruptcy is public and embarrassing. Though the bankruptcy deeply hurt his ego, it made him even angrier at the establishment. Did it cause him to change his attitude about money? Absolutely not. Because he was a doctor, he could still get credit. Robbing Peter to pay Paul continued.

Elaine was embarrassed but she had a role to play in this debacle. As was his way, John blamed the bankruptcy on everyone else. Elaine's expensive taste, the cost of the kids, and helping and supporting his mother were all reasons for the bankruptcy. According to him, his spending and lifestyle had nothing to do with these financial setbacks He worked harder and took other jobs, but his attitude and lifestyle stayed the same. We all know that the definition of insanity is doing the same thing repeatedly and expecting a different result. John's attitude and rationalization about everything he did was INSANE!

The cycles of peace at any price, resentment, and bitterness continued. The affairs continued. Robbing Peter to pay Paul continued. The arguments continued. The only communication that occurred was arguing. Eventually, Elaine became as stubborn as John and arguments brought no solutions just more bitterness and resentment. They had been living separate lives like roommates. They essentially had a marriage in name only. Elaine thought, *This is not what I signed up for.*

Elaine was becoming more depressed and disenchanted with their marriage. It felt like John did not care about her opinion on anything that mattered. They had no direction to their relationship or future. She began to live her life vicariously through her children and her friends. Her life at home began to settle into a rut.

Their move eventually occurred, and nothing changed. The house was smaller, but the same behavior continued. Not wanting to start a fight, Elaine did not ask how things were financially. When she did, the truth was never expressed anyway.

Soon, the bank came calling again. The usual Peter to pay Paul scheme continued until John ran out of money. The bank eventually foreclosed on the house. In complete and utter embarrassment, John and Elaine were forced to move out of that home into a house that was smaller than their starter house nearly 20 years before. And to make matters worse, it was a rental property. All of the kids, except the youngest, were in college at the time and they were all affected.

John became more bitter and angry. He and Elaine started to fight more. He refused to accept any responsibility for what had happened. One night when he got into an argument with their youngest child, Elaine told him to leave. She had told him this numerous times in the past but on nearly every occasion, he refused, stayed, and the two of them went to their separate corners. Occasionally, he would leave but it was usually to go to his favorite watering hole where he would throw back a few and then return home, most often sleeping in a separate bed for a few days.

This time he left and stayed away for the next three years. Staying away and blaming others, mostly Elaine, was just a ruse for what was really going on. He had another woman and was not only seeing her but keeping her in another apartment. Who knows how long that had been going on.

Shortly after John left, Elaine filed for divorce and started a new life in her own hometown several hours away from him. John soon could not stand the isolation and confronted his three oldest sons. He informed them that they would be financially disowned if they continued to ignore him. So, he basically bought back some ludicrous form of loyalty.

The kids stayed away but visited him on occasion, enough that he stopped his threats. Time went by, the divorce proceedings dragged on, and it was clear that John was going to lose everything. After three years, he couldn't stand it any longer. He either had to admit defeat, or at least some form of it, or essentially lose everything including his family. His behavior in the separation had far-reaching implications on all of his children. His hero bubble burst and his pedestal disintegrated under him. Never again would he be the idol that his kids looked up to. When he looked in the mirror, it shattered.

Though he refused to blame himself in front of anyone, he had to have some sliver of remorse. His apology to Elaine was a sham but it worked to bring her and the family back to him. She wanted the family to be back together and she was willing to overlook his behavior.

She and the kids moved back into an apartment with him. Elaine choosing to stay with John was a decision she would regret for the rest of her life.

Things gradually settled down and went back to the distorted sense of normalcy that it really had always been. No one really knows if there were other affairs, but it wouldn't be surprising. The marriage continued on and Elaine remained in despair, regretting the decision she had made to come back.

John and Elaine moved several more times over the years but again nothing changed. To admit the need for change would be to admit weakness. Weakness does not exist in someone who is self-absorbed, narcissistic, and arrogant.

Soon Elaine became self-absorbed and they both settled into elderly life as two self-absorbed people. Self-absorption affects relationships which it absolutely did for the both of them. Grandparenting was a foreign concept for them and they were isolated from most of their grandchildren which caused issues with their own children.

The last several years of Elaine's life were but a shell of who she really was. She eventually passed away.

John has become a bitter elderly man but refuses to change and demands to always have his way regardless of the havoc that it causes. He is beyond being able to admit fault to anything regarding his marriage or his family.

He pines to still have Elaine around. He misses her and wishes she were with him. He appreciates her more now. If only he had felt that way during his marriage. Instead, years were frivolously wasted at the altars of selfishness and arrogance.

Hopefully he can be an example for others to learn from.

CHAPTER 5 QUESTIONS

1) What are some of the positive aspects of John's character and behavior, if any? What did you learn, if anything, from him?

_____

_____

_____

_____

2) What are some of the negative aspects of John's character and behavior, if any? What did you learn, if anything, from him?

_____

_____

_____

_____

3) Are the positive or negative aspects of John's character or behavior reflective of behavior in your own life?

_____

_____

_____

_____

4) Are the positive or negative aspects of John's character or behavior reflective of behavior in your own marriage?

_____

_____

_____

_____

5) What are some of the positive aspects of Elaine's character and behavior, if any? What did you learn, if anything, from her?

_____

_____

_____

_____

6) What are some of the negative aspects of Elaine's character and behavior, if any? What did you learn, if anything, from her?

_____

_____

_____

_____

7) Are the positive or negative aspects of Elaine's character or behavior reflective of behavior in your own life?

_____

_____

_____

_____

8) Are the positive or negative aspects of Elaine's character or behavior reflective of behavior in your own marriage?

_____

_____

_____

_____

CHAPTER 6
SUCCESSFUL STRATEGIES TO HELP PREVENT OR DEAL WITH MARITAL STORMS

You have read about two different marriages from two different generations. Delores and Phillip and John and Elaine. Until about 30 years ago, there were no marriage preparation classes before marriage and no formal marriage programs to help married couples besides pastors or priests giving their perspectives on marriage. Pre-Cana classes, which have been popular and somewhat helpful in Catholic circles, have only been around for the last 30 years.

Priests present marriage from a religious perspective without having real world experience, especially regarding sex, children, and finances which are the top reasons why many marriages fall apart. In the Protestant and Jewish churches, pastors and rabbis are allowed to marry but still aren't exposed to society to a large extent like lay people are. So, their advice is a bit jaded.

What I intend to do in this chapter is to share some tools that could have helped both Delores and Phillip and John and Elaine's marriages during trying times. Marriage in Phillip and Delores's era and to a lesser extent during John and Elaine's era followed the model of the husband being the head of the family. He was the breadwinner. He made the rules of the house regarding behavior and discipline of the children, dinner and what time it was going to be, etc. The wife had a subordinate role and looked after the children, got them to school, took care of the house, did the shopping, and often took care of the finances or at least communicated to the husband what was going on regarding bills. Sometimes it was handled jointly, but the husband often made the decisions as to what to buy, how much to spend, etc.

This wasn't the absolute norm, but it was accepted by society even though it undoubtedly caused issues within the nuclear family––mom, dad, and kids.

Delores and Phillip definitely lived by the societal model as expressed above. At that time, it seemed to work. They were absolutely devoted to each other and Delores lived out the part of her vows which said, "for better or worse." Her devotion to Phillip was undeniable, especially when his health began to deteriorate. The following tools help couples to create awareness of the common pitfalls that we as humans carry into and throughout relationships.

A: Open-Mindedness in Expression and Interaction

Was there a technique or marriage principle that Delores and Phillip could have used? The answer is yes. The biggest issue they had when they were married besides

Phillip's health was their children and how they were handled when Phillip needed to take a sabbatical from work.

When he would take a sabbatical, he was instructed to go to a place with warmer weather. Warmer weather was south, preferably Florida, which is persistently warm for the most part. Phillip needed Delores with him to attend to his needs emotionally as well as physically. Phillip's sabbaticals were necessary due to congestive heart failure. The congestive heart failure occurred as a result of a heart valve not functioning properly. This would cause fluid to back up in his lungs which would cause weakness, shortness of breath, weight gain, etc. The extra strain on his heart was a result of the stress and anxiety that often comes from being a physician. Long hours on the job and lack of time for eating also does not allow for meals that are the healthiest. Patients with Phillip's condition are supposed to be on a low salt diet with no excessive fluid intake. Unfortunately, quick meals contain excessive salt and fluids.

Sabbaticals in warmer climates with less humidity allow for better recuperation. In a relaxed atmosphere with no stress, it is easier to follow the proper diet as well as to have the time to exercise. Exercise was first at a mild rate then increased to moderate. Delores was needed to help Phillip out with all of these important details.

Unfortunately, what ended up happening was that the children didn't factor into the decision-making equation.

They were young but there needed to be a discussion with them, especially with John who was the oldest. But, very little was said to them and they ended up being separated and staying with either friends or relatives. John and his brother, Michael, were only two years apart and to be separated from each other, let alone from their parents, was very traumatic. This lack of interaction would go on to create long-lasting bitterness and hurt feelings for both John and Michael.

The principle of open-mindedness in expression and interaction could've been used to prevent those problems from occurring in the future. This principle revolves around being truthful about issues and feelings and sharing them with your partner as well as other important members of your family, namely the children. Discussion may need to be altered to an extent that children will understand, but that doesn't mean that children should not be made aware of potentially life-altering decisions. There is a common misconception that children don't understand or aren't aware of behavior or changes in the family dynamics. To believe that old wives' tale is to risk family cohesiveness and the respect children naturally have for their parents. When children become adolescents or young adults, they will often surprise their parents regarding what they did or did not know during various times and situations in their lives. Feelings are feelings and they are neither right nor wrong, they just are. Feelings need to be sorted out and discussed at just about any age. Different viewpoints need to be heard thoroughly until each party is understood. Even if it takes multiple sessions of discussion for this to happen, then so be it.

Discussion should occur in a very non-threatening way, in a normal tone of voice, with all people involved sitting down maintaining as much eye contact as possible. Extremes of emotion, especially anger, should be avoided as it will oftentimes cause discussion to shut down. When discussion shuts down then nothing has been achieved. Whatever issue was being discussed has not resulted in any understanding. Whatever bad feelings existed before the discussion are now likely more intensified, making understanding harder to achieve. Distrust, anger, and bitterness start to occur and there is no desire by either family member to sit down and talk about anything. This then causes everyone in the family to be adversely affected.

The concept widely used in couple and family dynamics is called active listening and it is entirely appropriate to be reviewed here. Active listening requires all involved participants to be able to completely understand what is being said by listening attentively. Attentive listening occurs by thoroughly listening to what is being said. Each participant needs to be able to express their understanding regarding what is being said. If understanding is not achieved then repeating what has been said, perhaps phrasing it differently, is done until understanding is achieved and the conversation can move on. This concept is not only important with spouses, but it is especially important when you are speaking with children.

When Delores and Phillip went away for sometimes weeks at a time, there was very little open-minded discussion and there certainly was no active listening. John and Michael often felt abandoned when their parents were gone. They knew little and therefore understood little regarding the reasons why their parents were leaving. Living with friends and relatives is certainly helpful but it's not the same as having your mother and father around. Friends and relatives often have different sets of rules which are difficult to understand when you have gotten used to one set from your parents. This can cause anxiety, confusion, and often depression. Depression back in the 1930s was a poorly understood problem for adults let alone children. Friends and relatives are likely to answer questions and view certain subjects differently. Neither John nor Michael were adolescents at the time, and due to the inquisitiveness of children, they obviously had questions about what was going on around them.

For example, both were brought up during The Depression and inevitably had questions about why some people had jobs and others didn't, why some people had plenty to eat while others didn't, why some people had places to live and others didn't, and why some people had clothes and shoes while others wore rags and had holes in their shoes. How these questions are answered (the truthfulness of those answers) will often affect the attitudes of impressionable children as they progress through the stages of life. If truth is covered by opinion, which it often is, the child's attitude will be affected by that opinion. When attitudes are different among friends and parts of the family, it leads to confusion for the children. This issue becomes an even bigger problem when the children are separated and are being raised by different aunts and uncles, or different friends. It causes confusion among the children because when they are reunited with their siblings, they find out they have become the product of different attitudes as well as different parenting methods. This can lead to verbal and physical disagreements between the children, which often exaggerates their feelings of parental abandonment. That is exactly what happened to John and his brother Michael. Of course, premarital and marital coaching didn't exist back in the 1930s, but this concept certainly did. If some discussion had taken place early on, multiple lives would not have been adversely affected.

As it so happened, both John and Michael developed attitudes that caused problems in their relationships for the rest of their lives. Both felt that they had been abandoned by their parents. As a result, they had trust problems in their relationships. The times they were shuffled off to relatives were too numerous to mention. Their father, Phillip, died at the young age of 40 thereby worsening their abandonment issues. When he died, they were both left without a father at very young, impressionable ages. John was nine and Michael was seven. They were left without an important male role model in their lives. Delores ended up becoming father and mother to the boys and their younger sister. Yes, there were friends and relatives that tried admirably to help, but there is no substitute for a father.

With abandonment issues still fresh in their minds, their resentment toward women began to build. Their mother became the provider, the rule maker, and the disciplinarian. The majority of their friends grew up with fathers and were disciplined and advised differently. There is a male to male understanding that just is not the same as female to male understanding. They had been used to certain rules and attitudes from Phillip and certain rules and attitudes from Delores. They were used to an environment that had now completely changed. Delores was doing everything as one parent and discipline was coming from a female perspective.

John and Michael's adjustment was terribly difficult, especially when they went through puberty. We saw in an earlier discussion that the death of John's father would impact him in many detrimental ways for the rest of his life. It is regretful that the concept of open-mindedness in expression and interaction was not used.

B: Sharing Honestly and Openly Before and During Marriage

Being honest and open about your likes and dislikes and your opinions is very important, especially before you are married. Not being truthful in this regard only causes problems after vows are exchanged.

Unfortunately, John and Elaine's marriage was doomed from the start. I went into considerable detail earlier so that you could understand what a toxic personality John brought into the marriage. Many couples do not understand the importance of what their partner brings to the marriage. They fail to take the time to truly understand what the other person is all about. Dating and courting are very focused on physical attraction, and that is incredibly superficial. Physical attraction is generally what initiates a relationship and then couples get into what they have in common. For example, I like to go to the movies, I like to read romance novels, I like to binge watch *Grey's Anatomy*. Again, these are superficial conversations and give little transparency to what a person is really like. Dating can progress to a relationship but do in-depth conversations really happen? Sadly, the answer is no. Relationships continue and result in a certain comfort level. Spending time together is often done on dates while certainly enjoying each other's company but not talking about anything in-depth or deeply personal such as values, habits, conflict resolution, ways you want to be treated, attributes that are hard to change, etc. Usually, women are much freer with their feelings than men, so there is really very little constructive back-and-forth conversation. Oftentimes, how couples behave toward each other is modeled after how their friends act or how they were raised. Who were their marital role models? This is especially true with men and is often an extremely poor way to emulate a relationship. Men are frequently immature during the relationship stage, let alone while dating.

These days especially, sex is a large part of the couple's relationship before and during marriage. Unfortunately, much of what dictates how a couple is getting along is how they are doing in bed. Oftentimes, this ends up defining the relationship. Due to the significance of the physical relationship, truly critical character traits are not discussed.

In John and Elaine's time, a physical relationship was not as important. Though it did occur, there was an assumption that everything would be okay on the wedding night.

Questions commonly discussed were: Do you want children? Where do you want to live? What kind of house do you want to live in? How big is our wedding going to be? And although that is important ground to cover, it's not the conversation to really get to the crux of who someone is. Also ask yourself: Are they selfish? What are their attitudes about money and who should handle it? What is their stance on raising children? Who should raise the children and why? Is my mate easy to talk to? Do they shut down when certain subjects are talked about? Do they dominate a conversation or is there equal contribution? Do they drink too much and if they do is there a history of alcoholism in their family? What are their attitudes about friends and family? Is there agreement about how much time should be spent with friends and family?

Oftentimes, when couples come upon an issue and there is a roadblock for one of them, they think that it's not that big of an issue. They think that it will be an issue they will be able to tolerate, and that it will improve after getting married. Many marriages have fallen apart due to naive thinking like that. It is a false notion to think that you can change your partner after marriage. Such disagreeable behavior traits have likely been going on for years and are not going to change with the exchange of rings. Here is a good example:

As I illustrated in John and Elaine's marriage, when they started dating, John's ideas about relationships were already in full view. True, he made time for Elaine but the places they went and the things they did were at his command. His alcoholism didn't just start when they got married. It was something that had started when he met the drinking age. There was alcoholism in his family. The gene for alcoholism was there and passed from generation to generation. John exposed the part of his personality that he wanted to share with others. Whatever he wanted to keep hidden stayed hidden because he had to be in control. When Elaine dug too deep, it either caused an argument or John just shrugged it off. Their whole relationship was directed by John. Elaine knew about his stubbornness as well as his addictions to gambling and alcohol but chose to do nothing about it. She saw John as a good provider and a doctor who would be a well-respected member of his community. She wanted to be a part of that. She wanted to have children, and more than one because she was an only child. She didn't want that for her kids. She didn't necessarily want as many children as John, but she did indeed want children. Little did she know that after marriage he would pull a slight of hand after she had made it clear that she was done having children.

Elaine fell into the trap that most men and women do and that is that they can change each other after marriage. Personally, having coached and mentored hundreds of couples, I have never ever found that to be true. Couples think, especially the woman, that when the ring is on the finger, behavior can change due to the legal and spiritual contract that binds them together. That is a horrible trap door to fall into, yet couple after couple do. If the marriage survives, it is after lengthy therapy or coaching sessions.

John's behavior worsened after rings were exchanged. Earlier on in their marriage, Elaine wondered on many occasions whether she had made the right decision or not. As she would find out, that would be a question she would repeatedly ask after they were married.

What happened after their marriage is that many subjects continued to cause arguments and more heated ones than those that occurred before marriage. It proved that inflexible positions before marriage most oftentimes are inflexible positions after marriage. It is an absolute necessity that such obstacles are cleared up before marriage because the obstacles just get larger after marriage.

John and Elaine were part of a generation that as a whole were woefully unprepared for marriage. As a result, marriage was one-sided in a destructive way toward wives. True happiness and love were elusive. Couples stayed together because divorce or separation was not something, for the most part, that was ever truly considered unless you were a Hollywood socialite. Society ostracized you as a failure if you did divorce. Therefore, couples just stayed together because that's what you did.

If counseling or coaching had been readily available, which it wasn't, a better chance for true happiness and love would've been possible for both spouses. If attention to premarital attitudes and behavior would've been stressed, many unions would likely not have happened. Personality inventories would've prompted prospective couples to search their souls more deeply regarding what was and was not tolerable to them. Was being a good provider enough? Is the security that brings enough? Was the physical attraction enough? In my opinion, in most cases, the answer would be no.

C: Nurturing an Atmosphere of Love, Equality, and Respect

It is important to create an atmosphere where the goal is to be the best partners you can be to and for each other.

You are each other's best friend. Selfishness should not be a trait that ever enters into a marriage. True love means wanting the best for each other. In this way, we live out our relationship and achieve unity. We are called to give of ourselves completely, not partially, to each other. Doing so requires working very hard to not only establish unity, but to make it a daily way of life. Unity is a concept that is crucial for sustaining respect and love in your relationship during marriage. Later, we will discuss the differences between behaviors that are constructive (build unity) and those that are destructive (destroy unity) to your marriage.

There will be more times than anyone can count that will involve being angry and upset with your spouse. The key is to look inside yourself and to realize that this relationship between you and your spouse is not all about you. When you start to think that this relationship is all about you and what you want, then your relationship is destined to be on the rocks. What does it take for a ship approaching shore protected by low water and rocks to make it to its destination? The answer is that it takes teamwork and cooperation between the crew as well as the lighthouse master. Without a lot of hard work on both sides, the ship is likely to hit the rocks and sink. The same is true for marriage. If there is a lack of commitment and cooperation in the relationship, then the marriage is doomed to fail.

1 - Humility vs. Arrogance

It should be understood that humility is essential and constructive to a marriage. Arrogance is destructive.

The definition of humility according to dictionary. com is someone who is modest and has a low view of one's own importance (16). Someone who is humble accepts that someone else's opinion or way of doing things may be better than their own. A humble person puts other people's interests ahead of their own. The old adage is: "You can catch more flies with honey than vinegar." Service to others is the greatest form of humility. Indeed, that is what marriage is, being a service to each other.

Being humble means to hear your spouse with open ears as well as an open heart. It means putting the interests of your spouse and therefore your marriage first.

The definition of arrogance according to dictionary. com is oppositional. One who is arrogant has an attitude of being superior to others and it is manifested in an overbearing manner (17). An arrogant person is one who exhibits opinions and behaviors that are unreasonable. Their opinion is what matters and the only right way to do things is their way. Others' feelings mean little, especially if they are in opposition to their own. To be arrogant is to be inflexible and immovable. Such a trait is extraordinarily destructive in a marriage relationship and it has no seat at the table of what we consider a strong, respectful, loving, and equal relationship. Arrogance engenders no respect, no love, and certainly no equality.

One can look no further than John and Elaine's relationship for an example of the destructiveness of arrogance. John certainly is the prototypical example of arrogance. He went into his marriage with Elaine having an omnipotent attitude. Decisions in their marriage were based on what he thought was best. In his mind, Elaine was basically along for the ride, and to serve him and the kids. Her opinion only mattered if it was in line with his own. If not, her words were discarded as if they had never been spoken and the decisions or actions proceeded according to what he thought was right.

Here are some examples:

Take his decision to buy their second house. That was something he had in mind and was determined to do. Elaine was satisfied to stay in their house for a while until the youngest grew out of her room with her sister. John, however, would have none of it. He saw a house that he had always envisioned living in. It was a statement house. The statement was that "he had arrived" in his life. People would look and say, "Wow, look at John's house. He must really be doing well!" That would be music to his ears. The house was in an affluent neighborhood, just where he wanted to be.

It mattered not that Elaine was very much against the idea. It mattered not that Elaine had different thoughts about living in a big house. It mattered not that Elaine would be responsible for doing most of the packing to move. It mattered not that she would have to arrange for the movers. It mattered not that she would be responsible for most of the unpacking. It mattered not that the house was dilapidated, and the remodeling would be huge and time-consuming. It mattered not that she would have to be on-site coordinating the remodeling while trying to raise all of the kids. It mattered not that buying this house was not financially appropriate. John didn't care. He wanted what he wanted, and no one was going to stand in his way, least of all his wife who in his mind was not his equal. Their arguments over moving were loud and destructive. Every point that was made by Elaine was shot down like a burning airplane. She had no say; NONE! There was no love, there was no equality, there was no respect, there was no humility. There was nothing but arrogance and an attitude of my way or the highway.

As we saw in the story of their marriage, the decision to buy the house ended up being a misguided one that eventually forced a move to another house because of dysfunctional spending. It further caused a rift in John and Elaine's marriage that was destined to deteriorate their relationship.

Without active listening in an atmosphere of love, equality, and respect, problems can never adequately be solved, and decisions can never be appropriately made. When that happens, there is more take then give. Marriage requires a total commitment from both spouses.

When one spouse continues to give and gets nothing in return, the motivation and inspiration to continue to give decreases significantly. Intimacy diminishes. One partner becomes disillusioned and then resentment builds. When resentment builds, the gap becomes larger and then isolation begins. When isolation begins, communication becomes formal rather than informal. Interest in the relationship begins to wane and partners begin to lead separate lives and essentially become roommates. They then go from roommates to separate beds and from separate beds to infidelity, all from not following a ground rule that should've been made starting in the courtship phase.

D: Dispute Resolution

This may be the most important principle to adhere to in marriage. Failure to follow this principle can easily break up a marriage. This is a principle that needs to begin before the rings are exchanged. If as a couple you can't lovingly, respectfully, and without venom resolve differences of opinion before you get married, it's just going to get worse after you are married. The bond is just forming when you are dating and engaged. Responsibility is minimal until you take those vows. Once the vows are taken and your relationship is permanent, responsibility jumps by leaps and bounds. The stress of everyday life is now for a couple rather than an individual, which often is significant enough. A house, a car, children, and bills for the two of you are added stressors on top of your own job.

Without question, despite all of the preparation to the contrary, you are going to disagree with your partner on occasion. Some issues are minimal, like leaving lights on in a room. Some issues are huge such as spending too much leisure time away from home. In such instances, there has to be a framework to resolve those disagreements. How you react to your spouse when you argue is vitally important. Unless an argument involves an issue such as infidelity, which can be relationship threatening, there is no room for personal agendas. When you took your vows, you agreed to love, honor, and respect each other in sickness and in health, and in good times and bad. Unless those vows were taken frivolously and without personal meaning or merit, then love, honor, and respect needs to be in your heart ESPECIALLY when you argue! Of course, this is no easy task.

There are rules that need to be followed when you argue.

According to guruhabits.com, there are 10 rules for a fair and productive argument. Before arguing is initiated, there should already be a culture of respect within the relationship. The 10 rules are as follows:

1) Be courteous and respectful

2) Agree to a mature and intelligent discussion

3) Avoid the use of profanity

4) Stay focused on the topic

5) Do not bring up past history

6) Do not bring up hurtful issues

7) Do not criticize, condemn, or complain

8) Do not make the other person solely responsible for the argument

9) Limit arguing to a specific duration or a specific number of back and forth responses

10) Take a break if tempers begin to get out of hand (18)

1- Be courteous and respectful

This is a person who you have vowed to spend the rest of your life with. Your spouse is not a sparring partner. You are not a bully on the playground, nor should you act like one, especially with someone you love. Courtesy and respect allow no room for condescension. Create an atmosphere of truly listening, understanding, and empathizing. The reward will be worth it. Your relationship will grow in intimacy and trust.

2 - Agree to a mature and intelligent discussion

You are both adults, act like it. If you are not, then you shouldn't be married. Unfortunately, there are many immature people who get married. Equally unfortunate is the fact that lack of maturity often causes the end of the marriage. Being mature is being able to understand the issue that is being argued about, as well as having the decency to try and understand your spouse's point of view.

For example, in John and Elaine's marriage, John always went into an argument with the attitude that he was right no matter what. He always had a personal agenda to get across. He would only listen to Elaine if he felt that her point of view was close to his. Unfortunately, her point of view was mostly the opposite of his. In such cases, her point of view meant nothing to him because he could always rationalize his behavior or attitude about an issue. If she didn't agree with his rationalization, TOO BAD! John and Elaine would often argue about him spending so much leisure time away from home. John would rationalize that because he worked so hard and he was the breadwinner, he deserved to spend as much time away as he wanted no matter how late at night it was or how many days a week it included. This was incredibly immature as well as self-centered. Rationalizing poor behavior for self-serving reasons is pubescent at best and childlike at worst. Lack of maturity often goes hand-in-hand with lack of intelligence. It lacks intelligence to believe that you are the only one in a relationship that makes it succeed. Yet, John repeatedly showed immaturity and lack of understanding in his arguments with Elaine.

3 - Avoid the use of profanity

The use of profanity in an argument is the last-ditch effort of someone who no longer has anything of intelligence or significance to add to the argument. He or she is in a hole and is losing the argument and personally losing control. Disrespect takes over as does hyper-emotionalism and insensitivity. The person on the other side of the profanity loses respect for the person using the profanity, and whatever was achieved in resolving the argument has been lost. The result is that the spouse who was not cursing initially will also start using profanity or just allow the other spouse to win the argument. To have peace at any price, that spouse recedes, and likely communication will diminish. A gap, which causes decreased trust, unity, and intimacy, then begins to either form in the relationship or an existing gap becomes wider.

4 - Stay focused on the topic

Unfortunately, it is human nature that when trying to make a point during an argument, we attempt to pile on other issues that have nothing to do with what is being argued about. For example, if you are arguing about how to discipline a child, it is deceitful to bring up a different issue regarding your spouse that you believe to be a flaw. The topic of disciplining a child has nothing to do with how your spouse spends money. When we bring up points like those, we know it's wrong, but we do it anyway. It lacks fairness and all it does is either increase anger in the other spouse or cause hurt feelings, then the other spouse withdraws from the argument. Neither is a good outcome. Instead, try to get to the bottom of what your disagreement is about and solve it together. Don't fight to win, fight to understand. When you dig deep and fight to understand each other, trust builds enough for each partner to be vulnerable. When we are able to expose our vulnerabilities to each other and use them for growth, that creates a higher level of openness. You have chosen to build your relationship rather than destroy it which creates a positive cycle. The more trust you build, the more vulnerable you become. The more vulnerable you become, the more openness and intimacy you share. The more openness and intimacy you share, the more trustful you become, and the cycle continues. I can tell you this feeling is incredible. It is a feeling of love, acceptance, and pure joy.

5 - Do not bring up past history

Again, when losing an argument, it is human nature to bring up unrelated history, incorrectly thinking that you can better illustrate your point. As in rule number four, this is piling on and it lacks fairness. All it does is create hurt feelings which causes the other spouse to retaliate similarly or to withdraw. Again, neither is a preferable outcome. If the argument involves an issue that has occurred in the past, leave it in the past and deal with why it's happening now.

6 - Do not bring up hurtful issues

Bringing up hurtful issues while arguing is destructive. It shows a lack of love and respect for your spouse. It breaks the cardinal rule which is being courteous and respectful. It also shows that you are not keeping in mind that you are in love with the person you are arguing with. This person is your best friend. When you as a spouse pursue this line of discussion, there are deeper issues than just disagreeing. You are intentionally trying to hurt your spouse for the sake of your own satisfaction. If this is the case, what lies beneath the surface? Are you afraid? Are you resentful? Verbally hurting your spouse is never appropriate! You may win the battle but lose the war.

Say for instance you are arguing about a choice of meal for dinner. You're in a bad mood and had a hard day at work, and you're mad at the world. You decide that you aren't happy about anything. Your spouse has decided to try a new recipe to surprise you and to spice up dinner. You don't like it and you lose your temper and say something hurtful not realizing that the tone of your voice was being fueled by your bad day. An example would be a comment about being overweight which your spouse has struggled with for years to the point of depression and poor self-esteem. Yet, you lose control and throw it in their face. You have achieved nothing with this hurtful tactic except disillusionment and disappointment on the part of your spouse. This hurtfulness is difficult to repair and it creates a negative feedback loop. A hurt spouse will withdraw and not risk openness. Decreased openness creates a lack of trust. Lack of trust creates resistance to becoming vulnerable. Less vulnerability shuts intimacy down and the negative feedback loop continues.

7 - Do not criticize, condemn, or complain

The old adage says, "Do not criticize, abuse, or accuse until you have walked a mile in my shoes." This is appropriate in many ways but especially when arguing as a couple. There are many things that we can sympathize with because we have been through similar journeys ourselves, but there are some things we just can't empathize with because we haven't gone through them.

A blatant example would be a husband trying to say that he understands the bond the mother has with her child. A man has never carried a child for nine months and gone through labor or childbirth, so he cannot understand that relationship. To argue that in any way is to demean your spouse. Husbands to their peril will say that what they went through with their wives during pregnancy was as important as what their wives went through. Do not delude yourself into believing that. To make that point is ridiculous. Acknowledge and appreciate the difference as well as the sacrifice your wife has made to your life and the life of your relationship. As Guru says, "The objective of an argument is to find a solution, consensus, or compromise. Criticism, condemnation, and complaining poison the exchange and leads to a negative outcome" (18).

8 - Do not make the other person solely responsible for the argument

As discussed in relation to mature and intelligent arguing, John would often go into an argument with Elaine with an agenda. The top priority on that agenda was to prove he was right about the issue in question, no matter what the cost. To stop at nothing to prove yourself correct on one issue can often do irreparable damage to your marriage.

John would frequently use his educational advantage against Elaine to fight unfairly by using vocabulary unfamiliar to her to make his point against her. This tactic is destructive and condescending, yet he would do it time and time again. The goal of arguing should be to work on a mutually beneficial compromise. The goal is not about winning. Every battle you win underhandedly gradually chips away at the fabric of your relationship, that's losing the war.

9 - Limit arguing to a specific duration or a specific number of back and forth responses

Guruhabits.com advises five rounds per argument. If after five rounds no resolution has been reached, then go to a neutral corner (18). Nothing will be achieved in continuing to "beat a dead horse" except worsening hard feelings.

Considering the argument and reflecting on your feelings and your spouse's feelings is mostly more productive. Also pick a time to talk about the topic again, hopefully with a more reasonable attitude. Strive for achieving a mutually beneficial solution. This rarely happened with John and Elaine. Their arguments would drag on for hours with nothing resolved. Both would be screaming at each other at the top of their lungs. Elaine was mostly trying to protect her dignity, but on occasion would "poke the beast" against her own better judgment. Two wrongs don't make a right; however, there are times when you have to defend yourself. Unfortunately, Elaine was constantly on the defensive.

10 - Take a break if tempers begin to get out of hand

This is a corollary of rule number nine and is often what occurs when arguing is not limited. Frustration, anger, and resentment build with no progress made during the argument. The more each of these builds, the likelier it is that tempers will get out of control. This is a danger point during an argument. Unbridled emotion comes to the surface and irrational and regrettable communication ensues. It is often at this stage that there are deeply hurtful things said to each other. Things that both spouses most often regret saying because they said them in the heat of the moment.

It is also during this time that arguments can become physical. It is like playing a rough game of pinball when the top of the machine blows up the word tilt. Objects are sometimes thrown or even worse a physical altercation ensues and serious harm to one or both spouses can occur. Not only can this event be marriage-altering, but on occasion, it can be life-threatening and the authorities can get involved. If you or someone you know is in a physically abusive relationship, please see that they get help from professional sources. There is absolutely no excuse that will justify physical abuse. Relationships that have degenerated to this level are rarely repairable. The most important thing is the safety of the victim.

In closing this discussion regarding the concept of dispute resolution, ground rules are extremely important to follow. If rules are not followed by both of you, the issue will not get fairly resolved. The whole idea behind arguing is rationally discussing an issue and reaching a mutually beneficial solution. Despite personal opinions about an issue or topic, it is vitally important to bring LOVE to the discussion. If you don't love each other before you argue then your marriage has much deeper problems than whatever issue you are arguing about. A positive technique would be to hold hands during an argument.

Unfortunately, couples sometimes forget that they love each other when an argument occurs unexpectedly as a result of a snide remark. All rationale goes out the proverbial window. The desired result of an argument should always be a compromise that is suitable to both spouses. One spouse doesn't win, both do. Each side gives in a little bit showing that each spouse has heard the other and has felt listened to. The goal should be to do what's best for the marriage going forward which is best for both spouses in the long run. If an issue can't be resolved despite following these rules, especially after repeated attempts, it is imperative that an experienced third-party, such as a marriage coach, bring resolution. Couples need to take stock of their marriage and decide what they want for their marriage going forward. That's where I come in, the marriage coach. So you can become best friends again.

E: Honesty in Money Management

Statistics show that there are three issues that are at the top tier of marriage break ups:

1) Money

2) Sex

3) Infidelity

Honesty with money management is incredibly crucial yet often ignored as being significant in regard to the stability of a marriage. As with many concepts already examined, this should be discussed prior to marriage.

Each spouse should be paying attention to their future spouses spending habits, their attitude, their spending priorities, their interest in saving, and most importantly, their plans for the present and the future in regard to money. Too often this concept is neglected until it becomes a real issue. Often, one spouse is given responsibility over the checkbook and there is no regularly scheduled communication of the state of the family's finances until the problem is evident. Frequently, the problem has been brewing for quite some time and the spouse in charge has worried about bringing the issue up for fear of backlash. The problem can occur as a result of dishonesty, a mistake, incompetence with money management, or a combination of all three.

If you waited until your vows were spoken to discuss the concept or issue of how money is to be managed, it's vitally important that you sit down as a couple and get on the same page. Topics of discussion should include which one of you will be responsible for paying bills or if it will be a joint effort.

In this day and age for a variety of reasons both spouses work so that they are generating two incomes.

What are those incomes going to? Are there going to be two checking accounts or one? Some couples like to each have their own account. Personally, I don't see the sense in that. If you trust and love each other enough to get married, then why shouldn't one account be enough with two names on the account? In my opinion, having two separate accounts bespeaks trust and security issues that are bigger than money management. Having two people responsible for the finances can get confusing and disorganized. When that happens, mistakes occur, and arguments ensue.

Are there going to be separate accounts for bills and discretionary or disposable income?

Again, this is a matter of preference, but I think one account can suffice for both. Quicken is a computer program where monthly bill paying is set up to automatically pay the bill on a certain day each month. Some couples may not be able to afford the program or have the knowledge to use it, so checks still work. Additionally, electronic bill paying is offered by banks. In either case, whomever is in charge of the finances needs to make sure that there is sufficient money in the account to pay the bills. Bounced checks due to insufficient funds doesn't make for a happy couple, not to mention that it's expensive!

How is disposable income or discretionary spending to be spent?

In other words, what happens to the extra money after bills are paid? Couples can widely disagree on how to spend this money. Needs are the bills that need to be paid. Wants are things like a vacation, a set of golf clubs, or a new pickup truck.

It is also prudent to save or invest. Couples that do this are planning for their future or retirement. This shows a vision and it needs to be a mutually agreed upon effort.

What amount of money is acceptable to spend before needing to discuss it with your spouse?

This is so very important, and the amount varies depending on the couple's income. Amounts may vary from $25.00-$100.00 or higher depending on the circumstances. This is an amount that needs to be committed to. If it's not, arguments, resentment, and mistrust happen. The frequency of a purchase also needs to be discussed. For example, how often can I go out for drinks with my buddies and spend $25.00? Is once or twice a week appropriate?

What are our goals individually with money and what should our goals be as a couple?

This is a very important concept to understand and discuss before you are married. Discussing this at length will determine if you are both on the same page as to what you want individually, and as a couple. Dishonesty regarding this topic will only cause difficulty after you are married. It will also cause resentment that often is difficult for a marriage to overcome.

Set specific times when you are going to sit down as a couple and discuss money management.

It goes without saying that truthfulness is the key ingredient to successful money management as a couple. Dishonesty regarding this topic will eventually destroy your relationship. Hidden personal agendas or opinions on what is appropriate for yourself and as a couple regarding how money is handled are incredibly destructive to a relationship. Money, infidelity, and sex are among the top reasons why people divorce.

As a couple, agree on a frequency for discussing money management. Monthly is common because you have a good idea where you are after your bills have been paid. If you have a computer, print out the income and expenses which will also show individual expenses of each spouse. Each spouse will know if the other is sticking to the rules for how much they can spend. There should be copies of savings accounts and investments as well, if there are any of those. Each spouse will know exactly where the couple stands. There should be freedom of questioning so that each spouse has an understanding of the financial situation. Unexpected expenses need not wait for a monthly meeting and should be discussed at the time they occur. An example of that would be the need for a car repair or a medical bill. These expenses can be large and cause a change in goals for the family.

A good plan would be to have savings set aside for unexpected expenses.

Using John and Elaine as an example, let's see how money management should not be done.

You have already heard several examples of money mismanagement in their marriage. The overarching problem, however, was that John was rarely, if ever, honest in how he managed the finances. You will see in a later chapter how honesty and money management has helped to solidify a marriage.

John was very secretive concerning the truth about the couple's finances. He would spend money when there was no money to spend. Borrowing from friends was commonplace. He had his own ideas how money should be spent. John and Elaine never talked about financial goals and if they did, they were never on the same page. There wasn't an agreed upon limit for spending. John spent as much as he wanted to spend. Elaine would often get disgusted and think, *Two can play that game!* She would then spend money on herself or the kids, often not knowing how much money was really in the bank. Overdraft charges were commonplace which would anger John to the point of hiding the checkbook or forcing Elaine to ask him for money. Degrading doesn't go far enough to describe that situation.

Often, Elaine wouldn't know about a large or extravagant purchase such as the new house until it was already done. She would become disillusioned or withdraw. Neither is a good outcome.

There were never regular discussions about finances and if there was there was no honesty involved, mostly on John's part but occasionally with Elaine as well. The only time finances were discussed was when there was a problem that had already occurred such as when the bank foreclosed on the house. Regular and honest money management discussions would have prevented most of those problems from occurring.

Money management in the family doesn't have to be difficult or a source of frustration. Regular open and honest discussions done with mutual love and respect will keep both spouses on the same page.

F: Mercy in Our Relationships

How often should we forgive each other? Jesus answered, "I tell you, not seven times, but seventy-seven times." -- Matthew 18:22 (19).

Mercy is perhaps the hardest thing we as humans are called to do. Look at the world in general where there is little mercy or forgiveness. Country against country, ethnic group against ethnic group, political party against political party, person against person, and for our purposes of this discussion, spouse against spouse.

Let there be no doubt, humans are imperfect people and we all make mistakes. Yet, despite our own imperfections and a double standard of patience with our own missteps, we don't have the same patience for others or more importantly for our spouse.

It is a foregone conclusion that as a spouse, we are going to say and do something that is offensive to our partner. None of us is perfect. Often, it is unintentional but sometimes it is intentional. If we don't have mercy in our hearts for the ones we love, how will we ever succeed in any relationship especially when it is us who often need it the most?

Mercy is a decision that does not come lightly. It is often easy to show mercy, but sometimes it is not. Our spouse gets upset when we forget to do something such as take out the garbage or when we are in a fender bender that causes an unexpected expense. Forgiveness should be less of a decision in instances such as those because they are not a personal affront. The first is due to forgetting or neglecting a chore and the second as a result of a faulty decision or accident. When mercy is most difficult is when our mouths get away from us and we say or do something in the heat of the moment that is deeply hurtful.

Once again, using John and Elaine as an example, mercy by either spouse but especially John was hard to come by. When John incorrectly perceived that his dignity or integrity was being questioned by a statement, he would immediately hit below the belt. He would pick on what he felt was a personal weakness of Elaine's and hit her with both barrels. It was very hurtful for her to be called lazy. He would say to her that she had a very charmed life and had little to do each day while he was off working his fingers to the bone for her and the family. This was a personal offense to her because the accusation just was not the truth. At one time, she was raising five children and being attentive to all of their needs. She also cooked, cleaned, and did laundry. In John's eyes, the things Elaine did weren't really a job and he felt that her contribution to the marriage was less than adequate. For her part, Elaine would often throw John's drinking in his face. It was true that he had a problem, but discussion about it could've been in loving and caring terms rather than with venom.

Infidelity is perhaps the most difficult and hurtful transgression to show mercy for. It is deeply painful and strikes the core of the marital bond. The vows say, "I take you to be my wedded wife (or husband)." By saying to your partner that you take them to be your wedded spouse, you are promising them that your bond is forever at the sake of ALL OTHERS. Betraying this promise is basically saying to your spouse you don't love them enough to keep your word. It is morally obscene in the eyes of many as well as God's. Society it seems has become immune to infidelity and gives it a pass. Unfortunately, society has come a long way in the wrong direction. If you can remember in the book that most of us read in high school, *The Scarlet Letter*, Hester Prynne, the main character was convicted of adultery and had to wear a scarlet letter showing society what she had done. Obviously, that type of punishment was over the top, but now it seems we don't even blink an eye when a relationship falls apart. The fact that less than half of our marriages are successful and that the rate of marriage has fallen is a destructive demerit on society. It is just another example that the bond that holds society together, the family, is under constant attack.

Although something as egregious as adultery is often a marriage ending issue, we are still called to forgive one another. It is unlikely, however, that an issue such as adultery can be overcome by the spouses themselves without professional intervention.

Again, to use John and Elaine's marriage as an example, John had been an adulterer throughout his marriage with Elaine. He rationalized his behavior to himself before the cat was let out of the bag. John believed that although Elaine was a good mother, she was a poor excuse for a wife; she just wasn't cutting it as a marital partner. He felt like she disrespected him. To him, disrespect was not agreeing with his point of view on everything. It was Elaine not agreeing that he could live his life the way he wanted to and not be criticized for it. That meant he could stay out all hours of the night, drink when or wherever he wanted, play golf as often as he wanted, and most importantly spend as much money as he wanted when and where he pleased.

Context is very important here. John spent his formative years with his mother as the only parent since his father died when John was just nine. A female figure was his example and she could often be domineering. John came to greatly resent that. This was the time in society when women didn't have the respect that they do now. Women were not considered to be on the same social level as men. John grew to resent his mother's authority over him, and this resentment was just aggravated by the societal opinion of women. He had to work from an early age, and someone was always telling him what to do. He resented that because he felt that he had no control over the money he made. It was these resentments that helped to define his character as he matured through life.

John told himself that when he had control of his life, no one, much less a woman, would ever tell him what to do. No one would ever tell him how to spend his money. It was those destructive attitudes that defined his life and the resulting consequences.

So, in standing up to John, Elaine had never realized that she was helping John rationalize his adulterous behavior. John had affairs with women who idolized him and put him on a pedestal because of his place in society as a result of the money he made as a physician. These women lavished him with praise that massaged his ego, unlike his wife Elaine who had the nerve to call him on his mistakes. He felt that this was how he should be treated.

After Elaine told John to leave, he decided to stay away, and it gave him more breathing room to conduct his affair. He stayed away even when Elaine asked him to come back, choosing to lay the blame on her and his kids. His kids, he said, weren't giving him enough time.

Elaine became suspicious of John when he refused to come back. Her suspicions were verified when her son, Frank, found a greeting card written to the woman John was seeing. Despite irrefutable evidence, John initially denied the affair but eventually admitted to it, throwing all of the blame completely on Elaine. Failure to admit wrong was an outgrowth of his early years. Throughout his life, John had never dealt with his attitude and the subsequent consequences because he always felt that he had nothing to change about himself.

John and Elaine tried marriage counseling. However, in order for counseling or coaching to work, both spouses have to go into sessions completely open-minded as well as honest with each other. John was never a willing partner nor was he ever totally honest or open-minded. His ego would never let him be. Of course, the marriage counseling failed.

1 - Vulnerability vs. Entrenchment

According to dictionary.com, vulnerability means the capability or susceptibility to being wounded or hurt either physically, emotionally or psychologically (20).

According to Dr. *Brené* Brown in her book *The Power of Vulnerability*, "in our culture, we associate vulnerability with emotions we want to avoid such as fear, shame and uncertainty. Yet we too often lose sight of the fact that vulnerability is also the birthplace of joy, belonging, creativity, authenticity and love" (21). Dr. *Brown*'s research shows that we try to ward off disappointment with a shield of cynicism, disarm our shame by numbing ourselves against joy, and circumvent grief by shutting off our willingness to love. Becoming aware of these patterns helps us to become conscious of how much we sacrifice in the name of self-defense and how much richer our lives become when we open ourselves up to being vulnerable in our relationships. Through her research, Dr. Brown has found that people who are wholehearted truly live from a place of vulnerability. Being wholehearted, she further teaches, is a practice that we can choose to cultivate through empathy, gratitude, and awareness of our vulnerability armor (21).

To fully experience love in marriage, a spouse must be vulnerable. Love is felt by giving of oneself physically, psychologically, and emotionally to your spouse. If a spouse is not able to do that then true love is compromised. In giving of yourself, you leave yourself susceptible to being hurt. Love is not love without risk. To be vulnerable with your spouse is to share the deepest part of yourself and to receive that in return. The feeling of love is immeasurable and draws you closer to each other. Continuing to be vulnerable allows your love for each other to become deeper and more intimate. Vulnerability and love are directly proportional. The more you love, the more vulnerable you become. The more vulnerable you become, the more you love. Thus, love grows deeper and the positive feedback loop continues.

Entrenchment on the other hand, according to dictionary.com, is the process or fact of an attitude, habit or belief becoming so firmly embedded in oneself that change is very difficult or unlikely (22). As you can see, this is the total opposite of vulnerability. One who is entrenched can't truly love another. To be entrenched is to be so immovable emotionally and psychologically that being vulnerable is not something that is ever considered. They fail to understand how to connect with the depth of their emotions. Instead, they share surface feelings, never digging deeper to become fully known.

Being vulnerable is being able to take a step in faith to do what's best for your marriage first and foremost. Whatever is received reciprocally, which is hopefully a deeper love and understanding from your spouse, is secondary. Someone who is vulnerable despite getting their "teeth kicked in" is willing to continue to at least try.

Though she had her moments of being entrenched, Elaine was regularly vulnerable. She was often looking at the big picture––what's good for the marriage, what's good for John, what's good for the kids, and lastly what's good for me.

Elaine was vulnerable repeatedly. She went through the war with John again and again and continually gave in to his demands, his ego, and his desires. She gave in to the late nights, the drinking, the gambling, the "it's my way or the highway" argument, the finances, and ultimately to the often unpardonable sin––infidelity. Although she buckled to the onslaught of entrenchment repeatedly, Elaine continued to show mercy throughout their marriage.

John was forced to come clean about his affairs to Elaine. The hurt was deep to her soul. She saw the signs of infidelity repeatedly throughout their marriage but chose to trust. If she thought he was being adulterous, she would allow it to be a fleeting thought that passed.

As was his custom, John was entrenched to his role in the affairs. He believed even if the affairs were adulterous, they were not his fault. He felt that since Elaine was not a good wife, he was allowed to cheat. This was a rationalization based on his opinion, but as was often the case it was not based completely on fact. Marriage counseling or coaching was not an option during those turbulent times because entrenchment would not allow it. It didn't matter how many times Elaine showed John mercy throughout their marriage or how many times she was vulnerable to him, he could not show mercy and be vulnerable to her by accepting responsibility. He was court-ordered to move out during their separation. He was told exactly what he didn't want to hear and that was that he was an entrenched, angry, bitter and arrogant philanderer. Of course, he dismissed those words, never taking them seriously.

His entrenchment and inability to show mercy caused marital estrangement. During the estrangement, he was repeatedly given the opportunity to reconcile but he refused. The reconciliation would require him to admit guilt, change his ways that led to the estrangement, or at least compromise and be open and honest going forward. None of that was plausible to him. So, the estrangement continued and eventually led to Elaine filing for divorce. She did so feeling that she needed to protect herself as well as her kids who were still at home. John was bitter at the divorce filing and could not understand why she was doing it. Of course, he wouldn't. He continued to see his mistress and was essentially isolated from his kids who knew he was in the wrong. Elaine decided to try to go on with her life, she even moved away and rented a house. She was progressing without John and she was surrounded by many people who loved her and defended her. She was moving on with her life, content with knowing that she had been repeatedly merciful and vulnerable throughout her marriage to John. She had continually done the best that she could. She remained open to reconciliation, showing mercy, and being vulnerable, but he would have to reciprocate also.

John was isolated, lonely, and miserable. He essentially lived alone nearly four hours away. Eventually realizing that he had lost the upper hand, John decided that he had had enough of the isolation. He decided that he would drive the four hours and be vulnerable. He would sit down with Elaine and basically admit that he was part of the problem that caused their separation and his isolation from his children. He did not want to divorce, and he promised to change. Elaine made a decision in love and chose to believe and forgive him. She would not forget but she would forgive. She wanted their family back together also, but for reasons totally unrelated to John's. She was hoping for a new direction in their marriage. Sadly, that would never materialize. John would never change, and Elaine would eventually realize that. For nearly the rest of her life, she would rue the day she decided to take him back. However, she was at peace with why she did it; she had chosen to be vulnerable in an attempt to reconnect and salvage their marriage.

Showing mercy for your spouse is essential for your marriage to live, breathe, and grow. If you don't have mercy for your spouse, then it puts the foundation of your marriage in jeopardy. Mercy is rooted in love. Being merciful shows the altruism that you have for your marriage and that you are in it for a reason higher than yourself. The reason is that your union is an example for society, your friends and family, and most importantly your children to follow. You are paying it forward for society and to God, who needs to be the center of your relationship.

Matthew 6:15 states that God requires us to be merciful and forgiving to others. We have been given so much and have no right to withhold forgiveness from others (23). Mercy and vulnerability widens the window into your soul for your spouse to walk through, so that the curtain that is between the two of you is gradually drawn and you are one. According to Mark 10:8, "And the two will become one flesh. So they are no longer two, but one flesh" (24). We should strive for nothing less.

CHAPTER 6 QUESTIONS

1) What do you think of the marriage principles outlined in this chapter?

_____

_____

_____

_____

2) Are the principles easily understandable?

_____

_____

_____

_____

3) Do you see the principles as helpful to your own marriage? If so, how?

_____

_____

_____

_____

4) Can you understand how putting these principles into practice might have helped Delores and Phillip's marriage? And John and Elaine's marriage?

_____

_____

_____

_____

5) What are some areas currently in your marriage that could be worked out following these principles?

_____

_____

_____

_____

CHAPTER 7
PHYSICIAN, HEAL THY MARRIAGE

Among physicians, there is a common phrase that says, "Physician, heal thyself." Basically, that means to listen to the advice that you give to your patients. Or in other words, "Why should we believe what you tell us when you don't follow your own advice?" The advice of a doctor who is morbidly obese, diabetic, and who smokes carries little weight when advising a patient who is similarly obese or diabetic and is short of breath because of smoking.

For a myriad of reasons, the same saying could be changed to, "Physicians, heal thy marriage."

Though recent studies have shown physicians as a whole to have no higher of a divorce rate than other occupations, female physicians get divorced at nearly a 2:1 rate. There are a multitude of reasons including intolerance and stress related to working long hours. Prior studies have shown that the quality of marital life with both genders to be poor though no recent large studies have been done (25).

Physicians put in years of work and sacrifice a social life to become doctors. The college years are not characterized with "having fun" so to speak.

In making our way through training, many physicians develop an ego and it becomes a part of the baggage that we take into our relationships. According to webmd.com in an online article dated May 8, 2018, physicians have the highest rate of suicide of any profession in part from their ego, depression, disillusionment, and discouragement from their careers. The number of physician suicides is 28 to 40 per a population of 100,000. It is more than twice that of the general population. The rate of the general population is 12.3 per 100,000 (26).

In short, we are a very difficult lot to deal with in a relationship. Ego is not a very attractive quality for anyone to have let alone a physician. However, ego comes from a need to have the respect of others. Physicians have to be confident in order to do their job. However, their ego needs to be tempered with an attitude of sympathy, compassion, and empathy not only to patients but to our loved ones. Sometimes those traits get run over by our egos. Confidence is essential for all medical professionals, but it is especially important for specialties such as surgeons who make life and death decisions daily. It is hard not to have an ego when you are getting battered on a daily basis from many sides including the government, insurance companies, employers, hospital administration, etc. Is it a tremendous amount to have to deal with? Yes! Unfortunately, the wrong people, namely our loved ones, have to deal with the fallout from that frustration. Another factor helping to build our egos is earnings. Along with progression through training comes a progression in salary. In the initial stages after training, this salary progression is used to pay back student loans which are quite substantial. According to Jeff Gitlin of lend.edu.com in an online article from July 12, 2009, the average student loan debt for physicians is $196,520.00 for medical school alone and approximately $25,000.00 from undergraduate student debt. That's a total of $221,520.00 before even starting residency training (27). This is in addition to wanting to start a practice, buy a house, and start a family. It is an enormously crushing responsibility to have when you're starting your life.

Eventually, these initial expenses become less of a factor and physicians start to experience the fruits of their labor. This means a good lifestyle financially. With a good financial lifestyle comes an egotistical attitude. The vicious cycle continues as the money increases which further fuels the ego. An entitlement to material things and an increasing need for respect develops even if it has not been earned. The egos of some physicians lead them to see themselves on a level above others and as such, they believe they should be put on a pedestal. This false sense of superiority is also known as the "God Complex." It is a dangerous trap to fall into and can destroy relationships with family and loved ones, but most importantly it can ruin marriages.

Physicians often know that their dedication to studying can and frequently does make them socially awkward. After high school, the average physician continues to go to school and training for at least another 11 years. This includes four years of college, four years of medical school, and at least three years of residency. Primary care specialties such as family practice and pediatrics require at least three years of post-medical school training. Obstetrics and gynecology, which in some circles is considered primary care, requires at least four years post medical school and more if you want to subspecialize. Internal medicine, also considered a primary care specialty, requires at least four years to be a general internist, and more if you want to specialize in cardiology or gastroenterology which are at least three year subspecialties.

So, it could be up to 15 years or more after high school before a physician is really working. That's 15 years of going into debt, especially these days, and having spotty social interaction with people other than their patients and classmates. That's not a really good background to start off dating and certainly not a good way to progress from dating into engagement or marriage.

Most physicians are just wired differently. Depending on the specialty, some physicians have very little interaction with patients. Radiologists, anesthesiologists, and pathologists spend very little time, if any, in one-on-one discussions with patients because of the nature of what their specialties entail. Radiologists don't actually take the x-rays, x-ray technicians do. Procedures, unless they are invasive, are often done by staff other than themselves. Anesthesiologists monitor patients while they are under anesthesia but spend very little time with them before or after they are unconscious. Pathologists read slides, interpret biopsy results, and do autopsies for example but often don't see patients face-to-face.

In no way are these facts meant to besmirch physicians. It's just a statement of fact. Social awkwardness and lack of significant interaction can be more commonplace and make relationships even harder. From my own personal experience going through school and training, there was little time to even think about dating even if you wanted to. College was all about studying. Parties were rare and dating off and on didn't result in anything long-lasting because there just wasn't time for it. If you are shy to begin with like I was, that makes finding any relationship of consequence even more difficult. Throughout my time in medical training, I saw many relationships dissolve. There were various reasons for the dissolution but during training at least, the most common reason was lack of time to spend with their spouse. It takes a very understanding spouse, male or female, to be the wife or husband of a physician-in-training let alone a physician. The marriage, although it should be, is rarely primary for a physician-in-training. Spouses have to endure days and nights of not seeing their spouse, having very little alone time with them, and being the sole caretaker for the marriage responsibilities such as bills, groceries, keeping house, laundry, etc. Contributing 100 percent of yourself spiritually, emotionally, and physically and getting nothing in return is commonplace. When children enter the mix, if they do, it just doubles the amount of already existing stress. More responsibility falls on the spouse who is usually at home and that is normally the wife.

Relationships that start before training seem to have the best chance of survival. Couples hopefully know each other better before the real stress on the relationship occurs. Even then however, communication is key. The physician needs to regularly and exhaustively communicate to their significant other or spouse what to expect regarding the stresses to come. The spouse at home for their part needs to do their own research on what to expect for the future. It is very important for each person in the relationship to communicate what their goals and aspirations are going forward. If there are significant differences regarding how to move forward, they need to be settled before the relationship continues to progress. If couples are still dating, the relationship needs to be kept at that stage or they need to separate if there can't be agreement moving forward. If the couple is engaged, do not progress to marriage until this subject is settled. If the couple is married and differences can't be resolved, this is when coaching needs to be started and committed to regularly for the marriage to survive. I cannot stress more emphatically the necessity of regular communication before, during, and after training for the relationship to survive. Unfortunately, too many couples do not fully grasp how important open and honest communication is and that it is a necessity. They think that they are strong enough to survive without talking and continually using preventative steps to better handle the stress. Somehow, couples think their relationships are strong enough to weather the upcoming storms. Sadly, many are not as statistics prove.

Having been married 27 years and together for 29 years, I have seen the demands that medicine involves. There are similarities over the generations, but present demands seem to be more than when I started. Medicine is fraught with frustration due to, it seems, a concerted effort to degrade the doctor-patient relationship. Medicine, due to over regulation by a variety of sources, is robbing physicians of being able to primarily practice medicine and care for their patients. Electronic medical records as well as the evermore cumbersome demands with paperwork has led physicians to become more business and administrative conscious than doctors. For those of us trained before the advent of this change, it is very disheartening. For those trained in the present time, the requirements are no less demanding and relationship threatening.

In physician to physician relationships, one would think that the odds of survival are better. This is not the case. Attention to detail as well as the need for additional communication on future goals is even more necessary. Each spouse has goals in regard to their professional lives which makes coming to an agreement on marital duties even more important. Yet, often due to increasing time demands, communication is at a minimum not a premium. As a result, relationships disintegrate and dissolve. The wife despite being an equal in every respect to the husband seems to take a back seat when professional goals are concerned. She is the one who ends up working part-time or putting her career on hold especially when children come along. I have seen this happen repeatedly over the years with marriages that I have observed. This decision is fine if it has been thoroughly discussed and agreed upon beforehand. Too often, promises are made but not kept when children come along, and the topic becomes a major bone of contention. Sadly, the marriage goes into a downward slide and often dissolves.

Being a physician can be a very lonely profession due to the demands of the job. Time spent away from home including 12-hour days, weeks or weekends on call, and administrative duties, etc., begins to cause isolation. Frustration ensues on both sides and arguments happen causing further isolation and frustration.

Let's face it, opportunities to be unfaithful and reasons not to face marital issues are plentiful for physicians.

Healthcare in general requires numerous hours in a given week with the majority spent away from home. Many people in the field become depressed and discouraged. It is not difficult to find similarly disillusioned people in the field and a shoulder to cry on. Often, a shoulder to cry on progresses to a motel to burn off some steam. It is an all too easy trap to fall into if you're not careful. The hidden relationships continue and eventually meet with the same end, and that is the spouse finding out one way or another. The next thing you know you are served with divorce papers, hiring a lawyer, and discussing the custody of the kids.

While being married to a physician is difficult, relationships do survive.

Principles outlined in this book can and should be followed proactively and actively. No one has ever said marriage is going to be easy. Love is a huge part of every relationship, but you have to realize that you are both human. As humans, we have wants and needs that have to be met or certainly compromised. As physicians, if we can't control our own lives, we can't be beacons of hope for those who depend on us to be examples, let alone for physical and emotional treatment. So, I say, "Physician, heal thy marriage."

CHAPTER 7 QUESTIONS

1) Did reading this chapter allow you to gain any empathy for physicians?

_____

_____

_____

_____

2) Can you understand why physicians as well as other high stress occupations have such a high divorce rate?

_____

_____

_____

_____

3) Can you see how important open and honest communication is in all marriages?

_____

_____

_____

_____

CHAPTER 8
THE MARRIAGE OF DENISE AND FRANK: IN GOOD TIMES AND BAD

Frank was a young boy when he started thinking about marriage. Despite or maybe in spite of being exposed to many bad marriages, he could see the fairytale and he wanted it badly.

Although he didn't have a difficult time talking to people in general, Frank was a very shy boy around girls. He tremendously lacked self-confidence with girls and eventually women. Though he enjoyed sports, he really had no significant athletic talent that made him stand out. He attended a coed parochial school throughout the fourth grade. It was a Catholic school managed and taught by nuns. At times, they were very boisterous and overbearing. That worsened his already diminishing self-confidence and self-esteem. He did average in school but really never stood out. In the fourth grade, his grades were not very good, and he ended up failing math.

Frank's parents, especially his mom, wanted Frank to go to a local school which also happened to be a military school. His mom felt that the discipline and the small class size would improve his academic inadequacies.

Frank took the entrance exam and did well enough to gain admission to the school.

The school was all male which tended to exaggerate his poor self-esteem and self-confidence around girls. Frank entered that school in the fifth grade and was subjected to a lot of ridicule. School in many ways is survival of the fittest and what at that time was just "boys being boys" would today be called bullying.

Frank had an eye problem when he was growing up which necessitated him wearing glasses from the age of five. Looking back at some of those school pictures with those glasses, he felt that he was a child only a mother could love. The glasses Frank wore helped correct the visual problem that made it difficult for him to see but they also caused his eyes to cross. It was a humiliating problem for Frank, and he was more than good fodder for the bullies as kids can be downright cruel.

Frank lived in a neighborhood full of kids when he was growing up. He made many friends, but as usual you have to take the good with the bad. There were bullies on every street of the development. He had to wear his glasses wherever he went, and he was often taunted with the nicknames "Goo Goo Glasses" and "Four Eyes." Sometimes the teasing was merciless and the bullies would pick fights. Many kids were bigger than him, so Frank would be afraid to fight. Not sticking up for yourself encouraged more bullying so the cycle continued.

Frank's dad would tell him that he needed to stand up for himself, but the advice was never heeded.

Frank did not want for a lot growing up. He had a very doting mother but his dad who was a doctor was often away working or didn't get home until late. As with most kids, much of his time was spent with his mom who took care of his two brothers and two sisters as well as kept house.

As Frank grew up, he continued to go to the school that he started in fifth grade until he graduated from high school. Never at a loss to be able to make friends, he developed some long-lasting friendships. He had traits that were attractive to other people like his sense of humor and his generosity. Being an athlete of any consequence remained out of his reach, but he found other ways to become popular and to be noticed. He loved watching sports and would go to school games. On occasion, he would travel an hour away to Pittsburgh to see his favorite team, the Pirates. At that time, the Pirates had a couple of great players, notably Willie Stargell and Roberto Clemente. The Pirates brought Frank great joy while he was growing up.

Frank played intermural sports like softball and his dad taught him how to bowl and play golf, both are sports he enjoys to this day. He often played those sports with his friends which helped to cement his relationships with them.

In high school, he found that he had an interest in theater. The school would put on a variety show every year which was a pretty big deal. He participated in the show all eight years he went to the school and was the first underclassmen to have a role in the show from fifth grade on. He absolutely loved the show and really looked forward to the practices that started every January.

Academically, Frank improved throughout high school with encouragement from his father. Eventually he would graduate fifth in his class. Despite those strides, he still lacked self-confidence with girls. Dates in high school were few and certainly not memorable which just exaggerated the issue. Frank graduated from high school and headed to college at Marshall University with no girlfriend at home and the prospects for one in college seeming very doubtful.

Frank was never confident in the bar scene or with pickup lines. To him, it seemed more like work than fun. The more refusals to dance or to even start conversations, the more discouraged he got and just stopped trying.

Frank was raised Catholic and believed greatly in his faith. He went to his local church regularly with his parents and was more than satisfied and fulfilled with the teachings. He fantasized about being married in his home church with a big wedding before God, his favorite priest, and all of his family and friends. It was a dream that he would never let go of; it was equally as important as his desire to become a doctor.

Being a doctor was something Frank knew he wanted to do from the age of five. He came to see what a great doctor his dad was for helping people. Frank never thought about doing anything else in his life but medicine. Though never forced into his father's occupation, he was regularly encouraged by his dad who always felt that his son could go through the rigorous pursuit of becoming a doctor and never thought that it was unrealistic.

College years were forgettable ones to Frank. There was little time for relationships let alone dating. To many, college was about parties, dating, and having fun. It was about not missing out on what many would say would be the best years of their lives. Nothing could've been further from the truth for Frank. It was about hard work, getting good grades, preparing to take the medical school entrance exam, and ultimately getting into medical school. Did Frank date? Yes! Was there time for having fun and enjoying a relationship?

That would be a resounding, NO! Frank's dad would often tell his son that becoming a doctor was about delayed reward. Delayed reward meant that there would be time for dating and relationships once you made it to medical school. It was a hard pill to swallow but it certainly put a goal in sight.

Despite all of his hard work in college plus average and above average entrance exam scores, Frank was turned down by his state medical schools in West Virginia after his junior and senior years. He was devastated and felt like his dream of being a physician was slipping away. John heard from a colleague that there was a medical school in the Caribbean on the island of Grenada called Saint George's University School of Medicine. Many people told Frank to wait a year and reapply to his state medical schools. Frank did not want to wait and felt that he could get into medical school at Saint George's. It was worth a try. To wait another year and go through the possibility of being denied again was not something that he wanted to do. Frank applied and was granted admission.

Despite being a homebody and a mama's boy, Frank decided to take a leap of faith and travel 3,000 miles away to another country to follow his dream. He had only been on a plane twice and had never been out of the country, but to him this sacrifice was worth it. In August 1982, after saying a tearful goodbye, he started his journey. Three planes later, he arrived in Grenada, West Indies. What he came face-to-face with was worse than what he had been told or could've ever expected. He saw people in destitute poverty, living in one- to two-room shacks that were covered with tin roofs. These people were struggling to live day to day. They were being governed by a regime that had promised them an improvement in life that they never received. Their leader was homegrown, but he too was supported by a regime in Cuba (2,000 miles away) that promised him that same improvement for his people. Unfortunately, he had also been lied to.

Grenada had the most basic things and in many ways it taught Frank how fortunate he was to be an American and have the life he had grown up with.

The heat in Grenada was stifling and comfort was often hard to come by. Power outages were the rule rather than the exception. Water shortages were the norm during dry season and sometimes made showers hard to come by. More than once, Frank questioned his sanity for going to school on that island. Was it all worth the sacrifice? Fortunately, every time that thought climbed into his head, the answer was always a resounding yes. One night, there was no power; it was beastly hot, and his flashlight had run out of batteries. The only light he had to study by for a test the following day was the light of a bowl candle with the flame in the middle. It's singed his eyebrows as he read, and he almost grabbed a plane home the following day. However, he did not. He had a great friend who is more like a brother to this day and he helped Frank keep his perspective. He knew how badly Frank wanted to be a doctor and prayed to those sensibilities. Frank stayed. To say that life was hard and he was homesick didn't go far enough to explain things sometimes.

He would truly be tested the following year in October 1983 when Grenada became embroiled in an international incident. Cuban sympathizers within the Grenadian government, with the help of the Grenadian military, staged a successful coup and assassinated the prime minister and most of his government. Upon taking over, the head of the military instituted a 24-hour shoot on sight curfew for all citizens foreign or domestic. It was a very unpopular move with the Grenadian people at large and rumors that people were being kidnapped from their houses and shot were running rampant. None of the students were allowed to leave the campus and feared for their safety.

Most of them wanted to leave but they were forbidden to do so by the military government that had assumed power. The campuses were surrounded by Grenadian soldiers with AK-47 machine guns. After discussions with the US Embassy in Barbados and the Grenadian/Cuban military broke down, most of the students wondered how they would get off of the island.

The following day, nearly one week after the coup, they got their answer. The US military, under the orders of President Ronald Reagan, initiated a rescue operation to extract the nearly 400 US citizens, mostly medical students, from harm's way. Frank awoke to the sound of anti-aircraft fire near his dormitory at 5:00 a.m. He got to see firsthand the dedication and might of the US military and he was thankful that they were coming to get him.

For the next two days, he was pinned down and essentially held captive by the Grenadian/Cuban military with the first night being very emotionally exhausting. The students communicated with the US military with the use of the school's shortwave radio. They were told that it was highly likely that they were all going to be taken captive. They were told to keep all lights out and to make no noise. That was especially hard to do because Frank was in a room with a smoker who felt the need to light up a cigarette. He became so frightened that he fell asleep from exhaustion. Though they were surrounded, there was no move to storm the building and take them hostage.

The following day, they were all moved into one dormitory that was closest to the beach. Highly visible offshore was the USS New Jersey, US helicopter gunships, and F-14 fighter jets. At approximately 4:00 that afternoon, under the cover of shelling by the USS New Jersey, the military stormed the dorm and evacuated all of them. They were marked as friendly by the torn up white sheets they had been instructed to tie around their arms. While being airlifted from Grenada to Barbados, Frank was hit with the very sobering news that soldiers had lost their lives. It is difficult to express the emotions you feel when you receive the news that someone has laid down their life so that you may live. Our dear Lord Jesus Christ so poignantly stated in John 15:13, "Greater love has no one than this: to lay down one's life for one's friends" (28). Frank told the soldier who gave him the news that he would lead an exemplary life to show that their sacrifices would not be in vain. May God bless the US military for what they sacrifice for us on a daily basis.

It was at about this time that Denise came to know who Frank was. Frank was best friends with Anne who was going with Frank's brother Michael. Denise knew Michael and was just curious as to what was going on with Frank. Denise was born in the same town as Frank but they didn't know of each other for several years. She grew up in a neighboring state and was also raised Catholic. She too went to parochial school early on in her life and she eventually went to a private school also which was Catholic. That is where she met Anne who would play an important role in her and Frank's lives.

Denise was a very attractive young lady who had a particular talent for music. She learned to play the piano, organ, and the flute, and she played them all well. However, what she could do better than all of those things was sing. Her voice was angelic. As Denise matured, she began to play the organ at the local Catholic churches and she often played several times a day, several days a week. She sang as well. Soon, she was being asked to play and sing at weddings because of her talent.

After she graduated from high school, she went to the state university in Morgantown. She had thought of going to another school to major in music but that wasn't to be. While she was at her state school, she began seeing a young man who was from the same area she was from.

They started a relationship that progressed to the point where she decided to move back home and go to college in her home area. When at the state school, she began a major in pre-pharmacy but also took an accounting class. She decided after enjoying the accounting class that she would change her major to accounting and business management.

When she moved back to her home base, she thrived in her courses of study and ended up getting degrees in accounting and business management. Both would serve her well. Her relationship was also progressing. She ended up getting engaged. However, as her relationship progressed, she had some serious questions as to whether this man was indeed right for her or not. At the beginning, he was very attentive and well mannered. He would eagerly visit Denise on weekends and greatly enjoyed spending time with her. Unfortunately, as time passed, the young man (Bill) became comfortable in the relationship. It was as though he showed one side of himself in the beginning in order to lure Denise in. Once they were truly a couple, he felt that he could be comfortable showing his real self. That side was not the caring, attentive person he had shown; it was the extreme opposite. When Denise moved back home like Bill had wanted, he became less caring and attentive. All he wanted to do was stay home. If he went out with Denise, it would usually be to a bar where he would see his friends. Denise was expected to tag along and sit and watch while Bill had a good time drinking beer. Denise had noticed that Bill liked to drink; however, initially it was just when they went out. Soon however, he would start to drink at home.

It got to the point that all he wanted to do was stay home and drink. He didn't want to go out. If they went out, it was basically to be with his drinking buddies with the sole purpose of getting drunk. He showed little interest in getting to know Denise and her friends and family. It was as though he preferred to be a social outcast.

In all reality, Denise and Bill had very little in common. As I said, Bill was initially attentive and caring when their relationship started. However, that was not his true self. Denise had a goal of being college educated and finding a job of consequence in the financial world. Bill had no interest in being college educated and was happy to work in construction like he was doing and drink with his friends. It became very difficult for them to find things in common to not only do but to talk about. Bill did not stimulate Denise intellectually which she began to realize was a significant problem. They started to drift apart. More concerning yet was the fact that it seemed that everything they did involved alcohol. Denise enjoyed a drink or two but rarely, if ever, to the point of getting drunk.

Despite all of those concerns and lingering doubts, the couple decided to get engaged. Getting engaged should be a happy time, but Denise's engagement was full of trepidation which worsened as Bill's drinking worsened and he became more entrenched in his attitudes and behavior. The closer the date came to their wedding, the more Denise became concerned. It's not that Bill and

Denise didn't talk about her concerns. They did. The talk however was superficial, and the captain steering the conversation was Bill. Denise would express her concerns about their relationship and his drinking, and Bill would give lip service to understanding by throwing her a few crumbs and saying he would change. As it would happen, the change would be short-lived and he would quickly revert to his old ways.

Despite all of this turmoil, Denise was not ready to give up on the relationship. She succumbed to the cardinal mistake that many people make. She felt that when they got married, Bill would change. She could get him to come out of his socially isolated shell after they took their vows. Denise would be able to get Bill to cut back on his drinking problem after they were married. She mistakenly thought that the marriage would change everything and that everything would be better. As has been previously discussed, it is vital in the premarital phase of dating and engagement to become aware of attitudes and behaviors. Do not let physical attraction override behaviors and attitudes that are potentially relationship deal breakers because once the physical attraction wears off and resentment builds, there is very little substance left to the relationship. The statement, "I can change him (or her)!" is not a realistic expectation as many divorces attest to. Denise would live to regret the decision to marry Bill.

They got married but nothing improved. Bill continued to drink, and Denise continued to pursue her education. He had promised her things that he would not deliver. They lived in an apartment for several years and they were far from financially secure. Bill was beginning to verbally and emotionally abuse Denise. She began to lose self-confidence and her self-esteem dropped.

She persisted with her studies, but her fairytale dream of a loving and secure marriage started floating away like dust in the wind. Her evenings were spent sitting in their apartment while Bill was out until all hours of the night drinking. Constant fighting became the norm to the point that Denise threatened to leave. She began to berate herself for deciding to marry Bill despite his attractive traits. She realized that she had been a fool for believing that he would change. Doing this to herself further deflated her self-esteem; yet, she was not yet ready to give up on her relationship.

After Frank was evacuated back to the United States and eventually back to his hometown, he was totally unprepared for what would happen next. He was treated like a local hero for having gone through the international incident in Grenada. He was certainly happy to be back, but it was a surreal experience. He had done nothing to deserve any of this adulation. He was but a participant. The real heavy lifting had been done by President Reagan making the decision and more importantly the military who had risked their lives to get him out. There was an awful amount of misinformation being spread by the media and Frank decided that he would correct the narrative by speaking the truth. He went on all forms of media discussing the truth of what happened, even going to speak at his former high school. Eventually, he was invited to The White House by President Reagan where he personally thanked the president. It was a once in a lifetime honor to meet the president, but Frank having that spotlight came at the cost of 19 Americans losing their lives. Frank felt very sobered by that fact and he would never forget their sacrifice. He would tell all who would listen about the bravery and self-sacrifice of the US soldiers.

In January 1984, Frank returned to the Caribbean to hopefully finish his medical education after repeatedly trying to transfer back to one of his state schools but being continually rebuffed. He was rejected by his father's alma mater five times. Undeterred, he continued to work hard to try to fulfill his dream of becoming a physician. He was singularly driven and doing anything else in life would not suffice.

Finally, after the fall semester in 1985, Frank came to another crossroads. Money was becoming less available to continue though those student loans certainly helped. In early 1986, Frank's brother, Michael, convinced him to reapply to where he was currently going, an osteopathic school in Lewisburg, West Virginia.

Frank was accepted into the graduating class of 1990 and was over the moon elated. He felt that things were starting to break his way and that he would graduate from a state school. Thinking that he could get at least one year of credit due to his time at Grenada, he spoke to the school's academic dean whom he truly respected. Frank would never forget what he was told. "Frank, we want you, but you have to start over." Frank couldn't believe his ears. *Yet another obstacle to climb over. Were the two-and-a-half years spent in the Caribbean a waste of time?* he thought. The answer was a resounding no. A young and immature mama's boy left for Grenada in August 1982, and returned a mature man at 27 years of age in December 1985. Frank was more appreciative of the blessings in life that he had been given and it took the destitute poverty of a third world country for him to realize that. He became more aware of the path his life was taking, and He knew that God had a reason for it. Moving forward, that gift of awareness would help him deal with the incredible challenges that lay ahead of him.

Frank accepted his place in the class of 1990 knowing that the setback would be temporary and he would overcome this obstacle as he had overcome all of the others.

Frank was now 27 and felt that it was time to more seriously explore relationships. He had a long-distance relationship in Grenada, but the distance was too much to overcome and it eventually fizzled. Knowing that he had the stress of medical school to contend with, he still felt comfortable enough to want to be involved with someone. During medical school, he became involved in relationships with three women. Although none of the relationships would bear the fruit of marriage, they were all worthwhile in many respects. In those relationships, Frank began to understand what he truly wanted in a life partner. Two of those relationships lasted for two years and taught him a lot. The companionship of those women was very helpful in getting Frank through the isolation that can accompany the rigors of medical school which he was experiencing for the second time. He made lifelong friends during his time in Lewisburg and they certainly helped when things were tough. It's just not the same though as when you have that special someone to talk to.

What balances out the companionship is the stress and the fights that come with the needs of your partner as well as trying to maintain a long-distance relationship. One time in particular, Frank had gone to visit his girlfriend over the weekend and had an awful fight with her before he left on Sunday night. He had not studied for an upcoming test on Monday and he had an awful trip back to Lewisburg, getting a speeding ticket in the process. The following day, he failed the test. That relationship would eventually end.

He would soon start another relationship that progressed to an engagement. That progression took the stress to another level. This was happening at a time when

Frank was on the road going to different hospitals for training. Being engaged and on the road was more stress than the relationship could bear. Many of Frank's friends had repeatedly told him that his fiancée was not the right person for him; yet, because he was in love, he could not be objective. It finally took a separation as a result of an argument for him to be able to reflect and see what his friends were seeing. He learned the valuable lesson that when those close to you who have your best interest at heart see a problem but you don't, they are usually right. The engagement thankfully was ended and the decision, as he was to find out, was the correct one.

Frank went on to graduate in 1990, finishing in the top 10 of his class. Frank then started his internship in Warren, Ohio.

Denise meanwhile was nearing the end of her patience with Bill and their relationship. She began to realize that the possibility of salvaging her relationship was diminishing as time went on. Bill had become unhappy also and they began to live life like roommates more and more. Denise went to counseling trying to keep herself together, but Bill continued down the path of self-destruction. He had no self-awareness to see that he was destroying his life and their marriage. He began to resent Denise for progressing with her life. The more she evolved, the more jealous he became, and the less they had in common. Though Bill saw Denise advancing, she was not seeing it that way. She felt as though her life was stuck. They eventually moved into their own house after several years in an apartment. Besides the initial joy of moving into their own home, it did little to further their relationship. Due to the chaotic state of their relationship, Denise did not feel confident about getting a job in her field. Yes, she had graduated with two degrees, but Bill's constant belittling left her with very little self-esteem and hardly any self-confidence. She did odd jobs to try and keep herself busy, but they did little to help her confidence as none of them were what she really wanted to do.

Denise became bolder and did have some good friends who were providing a shoulder for her to lean on as well as motivation to demand more of Bill. She told him that unless he agreed to counseling, she was leaving. He ignored her until she was walking out the door with her suitcase in hand. Bill also had very little self-esteem and hardly any self-confidence. He relented and went to some counseling sessions just to appease her. He however did not actively participate in the sessions and whatever change of behavior occurred at home was short-lived. Soon after, Denise came to the realization that it would be better for her to be alone with a failed marriage rather than to continue with the misery of a relationship with Bill. She realized that she could lead that proverbial horse to water, but she could not make him drink. She moved out, filed for a divorce, and moved in with Anne in Pittsburgh.

Frank started his internship in Warren, Ohio, and instantly made many friends. Though he had a lot of fun with his new friends, many of them had significant others. Frank began to get lonely. He started a relationship with a woman who was 10 years younger than him. In 1990, Frank was 31 and a relationship with someone who was 21 was just not working. She was not in college and really had no desire to go to college and their interests were too dissimilar.

Anne, Denise's best friend, was married to Frank's brother, Michael, and she could see that both Frank and Denise were unhappy. Denise was dealing with a failed marriage and Frank was in a relationship that in his mind was going nowhere. Anne knew a lot about both of them and saw that they had a lot in common. Denise remembered that Frank was Michael's brother who had been in Grenada. Anne began to talk to both of them about the other. Their interests were piqued and soon each of them was asking Anne questions about the other. Anne began to tell each of them that they were made for each other. Each however was hesitant. Denise had just ended a failed marriage and Frank had ended an engagement. Though he was now in a relationship that was in his mind going nowhere, he was not eager to leave the security of companionship that it brought. After a lot of back-and-forth, Frank and Denise agreed to meet.

On January 11, 1991, Frank and Denise met for their first date at a restaurant outside of Pittsburgh. Right away the attraction was palpable. As Anne had said, they had a tremendous amount in common and Anne knew that they both wanted the same things from a marriage. Conversation came very easily. Before they knew it, they had been talking for hours about numerous subjects that neither knew they were even going to talk about. It was amazing for both of them and they were incredibly easy with each other. They took their date back to Anne and Michael's house where there was a party underway celebrating Denise and Michael's birthdays. It was a memorable first date in so many ways. When the night was over, they both agreed that a second date was more than worth it. The fact that they even got together for a first date was amazing in itself.

Since Frank was a young boy, he had believed in marriage. And he still believed in the marriage fairytale. The fact that he was surrounded by problem marriages growing up did not deter him. Besides becoming a doctor, marriage was the most important goal in his life. His difficulty with girls and then women from adolescence on just made him that much more determined to find the right person to be by his side forever. He wanted someone he could love who would love him equally in return. He would see dating commercials of a woman running into a man's loving embrace and daydream about one day experiencing that.

He loved the so-called "Chick Flicks," but he kept that to himself fearing ridicule from his friends. He loved the idea of the stories where the guy would eventually get the girl and they lived happily ever after. *Who wouldn't like that?* he thought. He grew up watching relationships that too often showed women not being respected, idolized, or placed on a pedestal like he imagined. He would often say to himself, *If she was my girlfriend or wife, I would treat her like a queen.*

While on some dates and in several past relationships, Frank went overboard and at times scared off potential mates. He was often too free with his feelings too early. However, over time and with several dates and relationships, he began to learn. He especially learned during the medical school years. He knew what he really wanted in a potential life partner and wouldn't settle for second best. Sometimes friends would say that he was maybe setting his sights too high. He would pause and reflect but always came to the decision that he wasn't.

Of great importance to Frank was that he be married in the church. That meant so very much to him. Frank was Catholic and the older he grew, the more important his religion became to him. It was essential that whomever he married be the same religion he was. Frank was still a member of the church where he was baptized. He had come to know the pastor there who was not only a well-respected mentor but a good friend.

At the time, the church's rules stated that if you were divorced or you were marrying someone who was divorced, you could not be married in the church. So, Frank really never considered even dating a woman who was divorced. Until, according to him, the Lord changed his thinking. He began to reflect on the fact that divorce happens for many reasons and most of the time it's not that partners just don't want to be married anymore. Often, there are real problems like abuse (physical, sexual, emotional, and verbal just to name a few) as well as issues such as alcoholism, sexless marriages, sexual dysfunction, serial adultery, and other addictions. Frank began to understand that he was not being fair, and he changed his attitude about not dating people who were divorced.

Wouldn't you know that the very first woman he started dating who was divorced was Denise. As it turned out, it was one of the best decisions he ever made in his life.

Frank and Denise's relationship flourished. They couldn't get enough of each other. They spoke on the phone regularly, saw each other nearly every weekend, and would sometimes meet during the week on Wednesdays. Frank was doing his training in Warren, Ohio, and Denise was living in Pittsburgh. It just seemed as though they were truly meant for each other. Everything just clicked. They went everywhere and did everything together. When they had time for each other, they were together in whatever they were doing. They would travel to places together and exhaustively talk with each other about what they wanted for their future. Their hopes, dreams, and aspirations were very similar.

To Frank, this was a dream come true. He had found his shining star. The key that fit his lock. The yin to his yang. He was 32 when they started dating and he was ready to settle down. Denise was a broken woman when they met. Her self-esteem was low and she had little self-confidence. Frank could see what a truly good woman Denise was. She just needed proper attention and to build herself back up after five-and-a-half years of being belittled and abused. He knew that she deserved so much better than what she had gotten. She needed to believe in herself and to understand her true potential. She needed someone to inspire her, motivate her, and catch her when she fell. She needed a best friend for life and Frank knew he was just that person.

Frank and Denise continued to enjoy their dream courtship. The more they were together, the more they came to understand how right they were for each other. Frank was ready to take their relationship to the next level. After a few months together, he knew that he wanted to spend the rest of his life with her. Frank never had any difficulty expressing his feelings for Denise. Understandably, however, Denise was gun-shy. She was still reeling from a failed marriage and wasn't keen on jumping into another one. She clearly cared about Frank but wanted her feelings to grow. Frank understood that and would be there waiting when she was ready.

Denise was so at ease with Frank. No one in her life ever really treated her like he did. He was attentive to her in every way. He was there for her on the bad days, which were numerous, and the good ones. He was quick to understand her and to bring her a card or some flowers. It wasn't long before Denise's defenses began to come down and she could feel herself falling in love with Frank. Try as she might, she could not resist his kind heart, his compassion, and his goodness. She began telling Frank that she loved him and how much he meant to her. According to the Song of Songs 3:4, "I found the one my heart loves" (29).

On February 15, 1992, at a showing of *The Phantom of the Opera* in Toronto, Canada, Frank popped the question and Denise said a resounding yes. It was nearly 13 months to the day after their first date. Denise could no longer deny that she wanted to spend the rest of her life with Frank. He fulfilled her in every way. He really knew her and accepted her completely. He checked off all of her boxes. They shared their hopes, dreams, successes, failures, likes, dislikes, values, religion, joys, fears, and a picture of what a happy "till death do us part" marriage looked like. Despite having failed in love once, she took a leap of faith and entrusted herself to Frank. A quote from an unknown author states, "Every love story is beautiful, but ours is my favorite." Denise expressed this to Frank and Frank to Denise. Their love and trust in each other grew by leaps and bounds because they understood each other.

To Frank, it was the fulfillment of a dream. One that at times he wondered if it would ever come true. He had to wait, but it was worth it. Frank had to pinch himself. He had found the woman he had longed for and it was oh so perfectly real.

After they got engaged, there was still something that needed to happen before they could get married in the church. They went to see Father Joe to look into getting an annulment for Denise. She poured out her heart to him about her prior marriage and its eventual demise. Father Joe's heart was opened wide and he felt she was more than worthy to receive an annulment. He strongly advocated for it and it was granted.

Nothing stood in Frank and Denise's way except the waiting time which they filled with planning their wedding. They enthusiastically and equally took part in that planning process.

Finally, the day of the wedding, November 21, 1992, came. It was a day filled with family, friends, and God. Father Joe was awesome, and he made the day extra special. The wedding was everything he had hoped it would be and more. It was just what he had imagined as a little boy. The video that he and Denise have of the day is priceless.

To Frank, Denise was the most beautiful princess in the world. She took a chance and kissed a toad like him, and he became a prince. She was angelic and radiant in her dress. He couldn't keep his eyes off of her. As Lou

Gehrig said, "… today I consider myself the luckiest man on the face of this earth" (30). The reception was fantastic and the honeymoon that followed couldn't have been better.

According to Song of Songs 6:3, "I am my beloved's and my beloved is mine" (31). Frank was Denise's and Denise was Frank's. They were best friends and trusted each other completely. As trust built, they shared greater intimacy. The intimacy in every way was breathtaking and life-giving at the same time. According to Matthew 19:5, "And the two will become one flesh" (32). It is a love that transcended more than they could've ever imagined until it was received in body, mind, and soul. When you feel that love, it is truly beyond words to describe.

After their honeymoon, Frank and Denise settled into married life. Frank was still in training and there was Denise right by his side. In the earlier chapter, "Physician, Heal Thy Marriage," we talked about how difficult physicians can be to live with and how they are a different "animal." Denise could not have been more supportive and understanding. She spent many lonely nights while Frank was on call, which was difficult especially being newly married. Frank however was quick to make up for missed time when he was off. In addition to Frank's training, he moonlighted to help pay off his student loans and during their engagement to help pay for the wedding and the honeymoon. It was not unusual for Frank to work 48 and sometimes 72 hours straight on weekends. Denise was always there to drive him and to be supportive. Denise had always been that way but she finally had a partner who appreciated the attention that came from deep within her heart. They had an intense appreciation for each other.

Frank and Denise were very committed to being as prepared as they could be before they took the vows that would bind them together forever. Denise had been through the very traumatic break up of a failed marriage and Frank had a failed engagement that nearly ended up in marriage. They were intent that those things would never happen again.

Father Joe encouraged them both to do a marriage preparation weekend that was put on by the Catholic Church. Though it was sponsored by the Catholic Church primarily, it was appropriate for engaged couples of almost any faith. Frank and Denise felt that they already knew a lot about each other because of the long, detailed talks they had been having throughout their engagement. But they both trusted Father Joe and were determined to live in a Christ- centered marriage. So, though skeptical, they went. When the retreat was over, they were so thankful that they had attended. Through their time together over the weekend, they found out that there was more to learn about each other that they would otherwise not have learned if they had not gone to that retreat.

We are new people every day because of life's experiences. Therefore, we continually grow. As we grow, communication is important to ensure that we grow together. Going to the marriage preparation weekend was a decision that continued to pay dividends for Frank and Denise.

After getting settled into married life, Frank and Denise talked about starting a family. Frank was almost 33 and Denise was 28. They were both ready and Denise couldn't wait to carry Frank's child. In January 1993, Denise found out that she was expecting and nine months later, Marianne was born to the ecstatic young couple.

During the pregnancy, a long-time physical issue came to the surface. Since she was a young girl, Denise had suffered a myriad of symptoms that no one could figure out. She was often tired, in pain, and had trouble sleeping. She had been to many doctors and tested exhaustively with no good answers. She had been given multiple diagnoses and tried numerous medications. Most of them had no effect and some had even made her worse.

During his training, Frank spent time with a physician who dealt with issues of the muscles and joints, a rheumatologist. Frank presented Denise's case to him and the physician was very familiar with her problem. He called it fibromyalgia. Frank drove home that afternoon and was eager to tell Denise what she had likely been suffering from for all of those years. Denise was ecstatic to hear that there was a name for her problem and that she wasn't crazy. It gave her such peace of mind. As he had always been since they met, Frank was very supportive and understanding.

To survive periods of turmoil in their marriage, Frank and Denise used the principles discussed in this book. Denise's fibromyalgia and the constant problems it caused her was an issue that plagued them for years.

In nurturing an atmosphere of love, equality, and respect, we are encouraged to be the best partner we can be to each other and for each other. Selfishness should not be a trait that ever enters into a marriage. True love means wanting the best for each other even if you have a difference of opinion. Those differences can be talked out if you keep your eyes on the prize. The prize is the continual growth of your love even throughout conflict. There will be conflict in everyone's marriage. That is a part of being human. The real growth of a relationship is to solve the conflicts together. Will you be able to solve every conflict? Unfortunately, there could be unsolvable conflicts even in a good marriage. The key is being able to accept it and allowing your partner to maintain their individuality. It is how you handle the unsolvable conflicts in your marriage that counts. Sometimes marriage isn't a 50/50 balancing act. Sometimes it can be 60/40 or worse yet 90/10. We can't predict the future; however, we must keep our eyes focused on each other instead of away from each other. Mutual respect for each other's feelings goes a long way. The important thing is to communicate feelings in a way that makes each person feel heard and understood.

2 - Empathy vs. Indifference

According to dictionary.com, the definition of empathy is to understand and share the feelings of another. To be empathetic is to be compassionate, considerate, tender-hearted, kind, sensitive, and last but not least insightful (33). Indifference, according to the same website, is a lack of interest or concern; unimportant (34).

Denise's fibromyalgia was absolutely horrible for her on so many levels. During her pregnancy, it affected her ability to do basic things for herself on a day-to-day basis let alone contribute to the marriage. Frank felt, on numerous occasions, that he was being "put out," meaning he wasn't being given what he needed in return, physically and emotionally. It wasn't that Denise was intentionally withdrawing or keeping herself from him, it was that she didn't have the physical, emotional, or psychological capacity for Frank. How could he be indifferent to Denise? The answer was that he couldn't be! It was not within his heart or soul to be that way. He deeply loved Denise and he would more than show her his love. Frank understood that Denise did not choose to be this way. She was not enduring fatigue and pain on a regular basis for the sake of seeking attention or needing sympathy. He felt that it just wasn't like her to do that. Frank and Denise melded together well and they were always there for each other with love and affection. Frank felt he needed to be empathetic and nurturing, not selfish and indifferent. He knew there would be tough times in the future where he would need from Denise more than he could physically or emotionally give. He knew in his heart that she would be there during those times. The exhaustive, loving discussions during their courtship, engagement, and marriage preparation more than made him understand that.

He knew that when he met her she was a broken woman. He knew that he would need to be there to help build her up in nearly every respect. Frank saw Denise as the kindest most loving, compassionate, and intelligent woman he had ever met. The bumps along the way to putting her back together were a labor of love for him. Were there times when they had to cancel going to parties, movies, double dates, etc., at the last minute? Absolutely! Being vulnerable and empathetic to Denise opened up a well of deeper love and caring that neither of them could have ever imagined. They really knew each other. Truly loving someone involves really knowing them.

Over time with love and support, changes in medication, and therapy, Denise was able to live a very productive life with her fibromyalgia. For the most part, her symptoms are now controlled, and she is an advocate for fellow sufferers as Frank has been to patients throughout his career as a family practitioner.

Frank finished his training as a family physician in October 1993. The month before, the Lord gifted their lives with Marianne who was born on September 22, 1993. The circle was becoming more complete. Upon finishing his residency, Frank wanted to practice in his home town with his father. Denise was content to live in the Beaver area as they had made many friends during their time in Warren and Beaver. Denise had no desire to move back to an area that had caused her so much pain, but she more than understood Frank's longing to go back to his childhood home and serve the people in that area. He had been repeatedly upfront about it. So, to take a step in love, empathy, and vulnerability, Denise agreed and decided to follow Frank as he fulfilled his dream. Frank could see the sacrifice that Denise was making, and his love for her grew.

Frank started his practice in a small town in March 1994. The practice was in a tiny renovated old house. It was perfect! It was just as he had imagined himself starting his practice. He envisioned himself as the old-time family physician who in bygone years started in just such places. He was very thankful to the Lord for the many blessings that he had received over the years. He had finally made it. Frank was a husband, a father, and a doctor. Had there been bumps in the road? Had it taken longer than he originally thought to achieve his dreams? Yes, but it was worth it. Nothing is worth having if you haven't worked for it. Indeed, Frank had worked very hard for it.

Denise was a superwoman, or so Frank felt. She juggled her life to make time for everyone and everything. Denise wanted to be an integral part of Frank's success. She had expressed that before he even started his practice. With her accounting and management background, she was a perfect fit to manage his office. She learned the business through seminars and was like a vacuum cleaner sucking up everything she could find on the subject. In the 10 years she was with the practice, Frank would say that she was the best manager he ever had. They loved working together and genuinely enjoyed each other's company. Denise handled the business side of the practice and Frank the medical side. They had repeatedly heard other husbands and wives say that they could never work with their spouses. To Frank and Denise, it just further added to the already deep bond that existed between them.

Frank's practice thrived and grew to be one of the largest family practices in the valley at that time. The slogan "We Care!" (Denise's brainchild) adorned the office, the business cards, and the letterhead. Frank loved being a small town doctor in practice just like his father had taught him. He and his brother, Michael, were now third-generation physicians and they took extreme pride in that. Time limits for patient visits did not exist. People left when they were ready to leave. Frank knew that getting to know the patients and their families personally was equal to, if not more important than, knowing them medically. Frank connected with his patients.

The sometimes chaotic life of a businesswoman, wife, and mother caught up to Denise. At times it was difficult to maintain the balance of it all.

There were never any female and male roles for Frank and Denise. According to Dave Willis from cybersalt.org, "Great marriages don't happen by luck or by accident. They are the result of a consistent investment of time, thoughtfulness, forgiveness, affection, prayer, mutual respect and a rock-solid commitment between a husband and wife" (35). In my opinion, Mr. Willis hit the nail right on the proverbial head.

Never once did Frank expect dinner when he arrived home from work and he still doesn't to this day. Frank fully felt that the work Denise did was equally important as his own job. When there was a meal on the table, he was appreciative. When there wasn't, he was fine with that and got his own meal.

Through the principle of open-mindedness in expression and interaction, Frank and Denise were able to keep many small issues from turning into large ones.

For example, when Frank came home from work, there were many days that he was exhausted and needed to decompress. In decompressing, Frank would often get lost in himself when he sat down in his chair. He was frequently oblivious to what was going on around him with

Denise and the kids (whose number had grown to three with the additions of Joan and George).

Denise spent a large part of the day keeping an eye on the kids. Even when she was working at their office, she was in regular contact with the daycare facility. When she got home, she was busy getting the kids settled down and making them dinner as well as getting them baths, etc. Denise felt that when Frank got home, he could share the responsibility of taking care of the kids.

Frank was in the Neanderthal mindset of: "I go to work for 12 hours a day, my brain is tired, this is too much for me to handle." Frank understood how wrong this attitude was and that it was unfair to Denise. He was just so tired when he got home that his concerns were wrongly outweighing Denise's. St. Paul said in Philippians 2:3, "Do nothing out of selfish ambition or vain conceit. Rather, in humility value others above yourselves" (36).

With regular discussions, always out of love and concern for Frank, Denise made Frank understand the unfairness of putting all of the responsibility for the care of the children--spiritually, emotionally, and physically--on her. Frank began to understand how self-centered he was being and even more than that how vulnerable, empathetic, and loving Denise was being. She was being so not only out of concern for the kids but for the marriage as a whole. The open-mindedness brought them closer together.

This necessary change of thinking on Frank's part improved the one-on-one relationship with each of his children that is so incredibly important to him today. Their open-mindedness prevented a mild disagreement from becoming a full-blown issue that interrupted their marriage.

After Marianne was born, Frank and Denise settled into their lives as a young family. They were really enjoying Marianne, taking her everywhere and treasuring the time the three of them were spending together. Frank was getting the desire to add another child to the fold.

The principle of sharing openly and honestly and the attitude one brings to the marriage came into play. Frank and Denise failed miserably to use this principle.

In Denise's past marriage, she had made a conscious effort not to have children because of how toxic the atmosphere was. The marriage began to fall apart not long after it started for multiple reasons. Bill contributed nothing to the marriage except for his paycheck. Promises given during engagement as well as during the initial stages of the marriage were not kept. The continuing emotional and verbal abuse throughout the marriage made Denise feel that it wouldn't be fair to bring a child into the marriage. She would be alone raising the child and Bill's lack of presence in the marriage would not make him a good co-parent.

Denise also came from a small family; it was just her and her brother. Denise's mother and father wanted more children, but it just wasn't meant to be.

Prior to her marriage to Frank, the subject of children was a rare but obvious point of contention for the couple. Frank came from a family of five. He had two brothers and two sisters. When he was growing up, there were always kids around the house to play with and to share thoughts with. A big family was what he was used to. It was what he wanted when he got married.

Because of her tumultuous prior marriage and the resulting severe hit to her self-esteem, Denise was very uneasy about being a mother. She didn't feel she was up to it and was very anxious about trying. After she and Frank got married, the excitement of being married to a man who was nurturing, caring, and compassionate got her caught up in wanting to have a child. After Marianne was born and with Frank's inspiration, Denise realized that she could be a good mother. Her pregnancy was difficult, especially with the fibromyalgia, plus she had "the baby blues" in the postpartum period. All of those things made Denise less than enthusiastic when Frank brought up the idea of having another child.

Frank saw things differently. He knew in his heart that Denise would be a great mother because of who she was as a person. In addition, Frank's mother, Elaine, grew up as an only child. She told him that while she was growing up, she was very alone and she had wished she had a brother or sister. However, just like Denise's mother, Elaine's mother just couldn't have any more children. Elaine had longed for the love and companionship of a sibling. Frank felt that if it could be prevented it just wasn't fair for a child to be an only child.

Before they were married, there was a difference of opinion. It didn't result in a shouting match, but the "arguments" left both with hurt feelings. In light of the fact that they got along so well in every other respect of their relationship, they just avoided the subject. Both felt that they could change the other's mind after they were married. In doing so, they made a huge mistake.

Nothing changed after marriage. Their difference of opinion was never ironed out. Denise had her feelings about having another child and Frank had his. Unfortunately, they weren't the same. They were gridlocked. Each was unwilling to concede their position to the other. The discussions really picked up in earnest two years after Marianne was born. They turned into shouting matches and the resulting hurt feelings on both sides were taking their toll. Frank never imagined that they could argue like this. As he would come to regret years later, he began to bully Denise into having his way. He became entrenched, indifferent, and arrogant in his way of thinking about the subject. Proverbs 21:24 says, "Haughty eyes and a proud heart—the unplowed field of the wicked—produce sin" (37). That seemed to describe Frank very well.

On this subject, he felt he knew better than Denise. He knew she would be a good mother to another child. He thought he just needed to convince her of that. He just wasn't taking no for an answer, and he would stop at nothing to get his way. It would be years before he really understood how using that tactic caused bitterness to build up in Denise.

Finally, after hours of arguing, and not fairly on Frank's part, Denise relented. Certainly, not enough of those arguments were with hands held, understanding, or no interrupting.

To keep the peace, Denise decided to have another baby. She realized that arguing was futile. As it turned out, getting pregnant was not as easy as it had been with Marianne. After a year of infertility, Frank and Denise began testing to find out whether either one or both of them were at fault in not being able to conceive another child. As it turned out neither were.

The couple began infertility treatments like many couples from across the country go through every year. After several rounds of treatment, Denise became pregnant. Though Denise was not initially enthusiastic about becoming a mother again, she was ecstatic that all of their hard work resulted in a pregnancy. By this time, she truly wanted another baby. Frank was over the moon. Sadly, the pregnancy was not to continue. Denise had a miscarriage. They were both devastated, but Denise's doctor said that there was no reason they couldn't try again.

From the start of their marriage, their Catholic faith was important to them both and God was put squarely in the center of their marriage. He would be reflected in how they lived their lives and how they would raise their children.

Spirituality is an important part of a successful marriage and it certainly was for Frank and Denise. When going through a difficult time, a loss such as a miscarriage can shake your faith. You have the opportunity to take a step in faith and grow closer to God or you can choose to fall away out of anger and selfishness. Frank and Denise chose to be drawn closer to His light. According to John 14:27, "Peace I leave with you; my peace I give you. I do not give to you as the world gives. Do not let your hearts be troubled and do not be afraid" (38). That verse is well-spoken and so meaningful. When God closes a door, He opens a window.

The couple decided to stop the treatments for six months and to destress about conceiving. Denise was fine with not continuing to try. However, she had promised Frank and she was not going back on her word.

The month they were to go back and restart treatment, Denise got pregnant. They were both overjoyed. Denise's pregnancy followed the same script as her first pregnancy. Some women enjoy being pregnant, Denise certainly wasn't in that crowd. Though her fibromyalgia wasn't as bad, she suffered from extreme weight gain as well as swelling. It just made weight loss after pregnancy that much worse. Otherwise, the pregnancy proceeded without incident and Joan was born on January 23, 1999, at 4:00 a.m.

She was a welcome addition to the family. Denise decided two weeks after Joan was born that she was going to return to work. It was a decision that would have lasting and devastating consequences for her. Denise never skipped a beat at work. She continued to manage the practice as she had before, and it was getting larger. So large that they moved the practice to another building with more space. Denise facilitated the whole move in addition to managing the business, the employees, the house, and the kids.

Nine months after Joan was born, Denise began to crash mentally and physically. She became unable to sleep and her appetite decreased considerably. She started to experience extreme mood swings but was depressed for most of the time. She began to get very anxious before bedtime fearing that she would be unable to sleep. As one might expect, Denise's anxiety grew considerably worse. She became unable to concentrate on even the smallest things. Taking care of herself let alone work and the kids had become a daunting chore. Denise was becoming overwhelmed by life itself. What's worse is that she began having awful thoughts about Joan. On more than one occasion, she feared hurting her. Denise was horrified that such thoughts could ever enter her mind and she beat herself up even more for having them. She began to have suicidal thoughts as well.

One day at work, Frank saw the abysmal state Denise was in and he had had enough. He asked Denise if she could drive herself home and she said she could. She went home and got into bed. Frank shortened his day and then went to the store for a few things including flowers and a greeting card. This was a crisis in their marriage that had come on unexpectedly. It would certainly test the strength of their bond. Frank knew a lot about multiple fields of medicine which he was required to know as a family practitioner. As he would say, "Family docs need to know a little about a lot and specialists need to know a lot about a little!" Frank knew Denise's diagnosis was above him and he needed some objectivity and some help. Thankfully, he had a friend who was a psychiatrist and he sought her help. He and Denise went to see her, and they found out that Denise was one of three million women annually diagnosed with postpartum depression (39). Denise was placed on medication as well as given advice to be off of work for a few months. Frank was determined to see Denise through the hellish experience she was in. He was going to do whatever was necessary to help her through that period.

They used nearly all of the principles that they had been following to get Denise through that experience. Nurturing an atmosphere of love and equality and respect was so very important during that time.

Denise was at the lowest she had ever been. She was incredibly vulnerable, physically and emotionally, and Frank could sense that. She needed him more than she had ever needed him before in the seven years they had been married.

There were days that Denise couldn't eat, and Frank would be there mixing up a milkshake with Carnation Instant Breakfast, ice cream, and eggs. Denise dutifully drank it down. She was unable to care for Joan, so Frank hired a very dear friend of theirs named Kim to stay in the house and care for Joan, especially at night, so that Denise could get the sleep she so desperately needed.

The healing process was long and difficult. Denise had a lot of anger because of the way she was feeling. She would ask, "Why me?" There was really no good answer for that question. The anger would often spill over onto Frank and it took all he had within himself not to strike back. He kept the rules for arguing in the back of his head at all times. With all she was dealing with, those rules were the farthest thing from Denise's mind. Frank was sympathetic toward her and he knew full well that she didn't choose to feel the way she was feeling. Frank knew that there was probably some pent-up hostility toward him because of his insistence on having more children. He knew she was venting and that the frustration was hitting her from so many sides. Denise was giving all she could give, and he knew it. Frank rode the wave of emotions and with God and family, helped Denise get through it.

After many months of medicine as well as support from numerous sources, Denise finally reached the other side of the hill called postpartum depression. She then became an advocate for women with PPD and was a shoulder to cry on for many women who sought her out for her advice.

Denise eventually went back to work and pushed the practice forward, all the while dealing with new rules and regulations that were flooding the medical field which was influencing the practice of medicine.

Frank had many issues that dealt with medicine, including the loss of patients. He was very happy being an "old time" family doc. He still made house calls and made it a point to be accessible to his patients even in their darkest hours. On more occasions than can be counted, Frank was present at a patient's deathbed, being strong. He felt that he needed to be the voice of reason when family members were being overwhelmed with grief and emotion. More than once, Denise was there with him being equally as comforting.

On many occasions, Frank had the privilege of eulogizing his patients. To him it was an honor. It was the least he could do for people that had entrusted him with their care. The eulogies took a toll on Frank. In being strong, he had to suppress his emotions, making it difficult to show emotion when he wanted to. It is an issue he still deals with today. Frank and Denise were settling into life with their kids and the thriving family practice they had built together. It was a labor of love and it cemented the love that they had for each other.

In 2001, on September 11 as a matter of fact, they moved into a larger house because of their larger family. That day was a double-edged sword. There was the joy of moving into a new and more spacious house, yet there was the devastation that was happening in New York, Virginia, and Pennsylvania. That day will always be of twofold significance to them.

The house that they had bought needed so much work. They enjoyed fixing it up and did some of the work themselves. While they were fixing it up, Frank became very interested in a painter by the name of Thomas Kinkade. He was very impressed by his style in the use of light. He and Denise bought a couple of the paintings that still adorn their house. Frank wasn't satisfied with that, however. He saw other Thomas Kincaid paintings that he liked, and he wanted to buy more. Ever the penny pincher and the realist, Denise strongly objected and favored waiting. Frank felt that Denise wasn't being fair. He had it in his mind that he would go ahead and buy the paintings. He felt that once she saw what they looked like, she would be happy that he bought them. Frank knew full well that the finances of their marriage were based on the principle of fairness in the management of money. Yet, he ignored that and decided he knew best. He went ahead and ordered three more paintings. When they came to the house, Denise was not happy to see them. She was furious and she had every right to be. They had set a limit regarding the cost of a purchase before it needed to be discussed with the other spouse. Frank went way above that limit. Denise was hurt. He knew that he was in the wrong so there was very little argument. The paintings for the most part went back. Since then, except for an occasional disagreement, Denise handles the money management and it has suited them well.

In 2002, three years after Joan was born, Denise became pregnant with George. She had adjusted to life with Marianne and Joan. She was pregnant at an advanced age of 38 but otherwise, she took the pregnancy in stride. On February 28, 2003, George was born. Frank loved his girls dearly, but he really wanted to have a son and the Lord gifted him with one.

Frank was an avid sports fan and enjoyed being able to teach his son about sports from a very young age.

Frank and Denise felt truly blessed. They were gifted with three children and were very active in their lives. They were blessed with a very strong and loving marriage. It was made strong due to effort. They constantly communicated about every facet of their marriage. Denise decided to step away from Frank's practice after George was born to spend more time raising him. She had devoted so much of her time working long days at the expense of spending time with Marianne and Joan.

Denise had what she called "Mommy Guilt." She felt bad about not being able to be there for the two girls like she wanted to be when they were young. She wanted to be the best mother she could be but like so many mothers made the choice to work.

Frank and Denise were lucky to have had a very dependable daycare that all three of their children were a part of. They also had Denise's mother, Irene, who was very dependable, caring, and life-giving when the kids needed care, love, and support. Because of Irene, the kids had a wonderful grandparent experience. Her dedication also allowed Frank and Denise to spend time with each other on their marriage.

The couple always promised that they would put their marriage first and in doing so God was also first. They felt that by placing their marriage first and keeping it front and center in their thoughts, they could better raise their children. Keeping their marriage first meant taking breaks, by travelling and getting away, to recharge their relationship. The day-to-day grind of working as well as raising the kids could cause both physical and mental exhaustion. So, Frank and Denise tried to make a regular habit of "getting away" every three to four months. Getting away can mean a vacation, if it's affordable, a weekend nearby at a bed and breakfast, or just visiting friends or relatives. Whatever or where ever, it is time to spend exclusively on each other. They called this alone time. This needs to be done without children being with you. If they are, there is no way you can spend time being present with each other communicating physically and emotionally. This is not to say that spending time together shouldn't be done consistently during the week. Date nights help and of course so does communicating regularly like we have discussed. Those things need to be done. However, time and space to recharge your relationship is essential for good marriage health. This time reminds you why you got married, why you are still married, and why you continue to choose to be married. Because Frank and Denise have always made time for recharging their marriage their relationship has survived. Also, their children and their relationship with them has thrived. They have been blessed to spend time together sharing in the many different places they have traveled. It has been time they have deeply treasured, uniting both of them.

When Denise left her job, Frank continued in the practice, but it was never the same without her. He sold his practice and became an employee of several different hospitals. He missed Denise's presence at the practice deeply. Previously, when Frank was frustrated at the end of an emotionally charged day, Denise was always there with empathy because she knew and understood the rigors of the practice of medicine. When she left and began to focus on their newborn, George, as well as the rest of the children, that became her main focus which was understandable. Medicine continued to change by leaps and bounds and according to Frank and many other physicians, not in a good way. As rules and regulations in the practice of medicine changed, it seemed like they were creating distance in the doctor-patient relationship. In doing so, "old time" family docs like Frank were being passed by. He became progressively frustrated as well as stressed. Medicine was becoming more about money and numbers rather than relationships.

Denise was aware of the changes, but they were no longer her biggest focus and Frank missed that. He would always regret that loss.

Frank and Denise continued to be tested as they went forward in their marriage and the strength of the relationship they had worked on so hard always won out. Nothing, however, would ever test them like what they would see in the future.

In December of 2012, Frank gave up his family practice of nearly 20 years to try a new type of medicine called urgent care. He started urgent care in January of 2013. From nearly the start, Frank regretted his decision. Where he worked was totally foreign to anything he was used to. His style of practice was to see patients, get to know them, then diagnose and treat them. This new environment was about seeing people as quickly as possible and moving onto the next patient, spending as little as five minutes with them sometimes. Simultaneously, you were expected to provide the same service as a visit of 15-30 minutes. That was extremely difficult to say the least. The "treat 'em and street 'em" mentality was more than Frank could tolerate after a while. He soon looked into getting back to his true love which was family practice. After looking for nearly a year and becoming more disenchanted where he was working, Frank finally found a position in southeastern Ohio where he would be asked to start a new practice.

Frank was more than ready for the challenge. He started his new practice on July 1, 2014, and was warmly welcomed by the community. He was ecstatic to be back in family practice again. He got busy quickly as the area was very much in need of a new family practitioner. The job was an hour away from his home, but the drive did not bother him because he enjoyed what he was doing and the people he was treating. Frank became widely known in the community for his caring and compassion as well as going the extra mile to treat patients. His practice and staff grew. He was involved in the community and felt he was returning to his roots as a family doctor.

It was always Frank's feeling that physicians should step in to fill gaps in care if they have the ability. Early in his career, he began to see patients from all walks of life that were suffering debilitating pain. Their accessibility to treatment was horrendous. The number of physicians available to treat pain was far less than what was needed to handle the number of patients who were truly suffering. The Hippocratic Oath says to "First, do no harm." To Frank, to not help was to do harm. He studied for and obtained an extra certification to treat pain. He also took many continuing education courses. In preparing to treat patients with acute and chronic pain in his practice, he set up many protocols to assure himself as well as others that he was doing the right things. He did an externship in Tennessee and used their recommendations to add to what he was already doing. He felt good about what he was doing and believed that he was genuinely helping people.

During the time that he was treating patient's chronic pain, he had a number of charts reviewed by the medical boards. As the saying goes, "Fools rush in where angels fear to tread." Many physicians were rightfully hesitant to treat patients with chronic pain and steered clear of it, but Frank's heart went out to those patients and he was sympathetic to their plight. Pain was something that legislators initially felt needed to be aggressively treated. Indeed, it was a right that patients had. Pain was actually called the fifth vital sign and physicians were required to ask patients about their level of pain in and out of the hospital.

Eventually, however, the tide turned and the practice of pain became progressively regulated. Pain is difficult to prove and is subjective to each patient. Objective tests like x-rays and bloodwork can only help a physician so much in determining the accuracy of a patient's level of pain. As in many facets of medicine, physicians rely on the honesty of patients.

In reflecting on their marriage, Frank and Denise talked a lot. She began to reveal issues that were very hurtful to him. Then she said that there were many times during their marriage that she felt like Frank had bullied her. Not physically, but in the context of dispute resolution. Denise said that there were numerous times that she would settle an argument and give him his way just to keep the peace. Peace at any price. And the price was their intimacy as a couple. That happened during major events in their marriage. Frank wanted to move back to his home town, but she didn't. He wanted to have more kids, but she wanted only one. Earlier in their marriage, he often put Denise in the middle of arguments with his family. Frank was dumbfounded. He was distraught that Denise felt he was a bully. He had deceived himself into thinking that he was being reasonable during their discussions. He felt that he had been abiding by the principles of dispute resolution. However, he had not been.

Frank had shared with Denise about not wanting to go to bed angry. He spoke with her about spouses whose last remembrances of their other spouse before they passed was an argument. It was just an awful burden to have to bear. So, there were nights that they would stay up all night trying to settle a disagreement with Frank trying what he thought was being nice. However, he was being arrogant and a bully. He thought he knew what was best for Denise. In doing so, he broke the cardinal rule in dispute resolution and that was to be courteous and respectful. Denise would eventually give in because she didn't want to keep arguing. She really did love Frank because he was such a great spouse in so many ways. Slowly, she began to build resentment toward Frank because of his bullying. She never brought it up to him out of fear of being bullied. So, this went on for a period of time with Frank being none the wiser. It took his self-esteem being scraped on the ground and him being tremendously vulnerable before he could really reflect and listen to Denise about what a total ass he had been to her.

Frank poured out his heart to Denise in a detailed letter of apology. He had unintentionally made Denise feel that she could not be open and honest with him out of fear. Many times, we fear communicating with our spouse because we are afraid of their reaction to our feelings. As a result, we keep those feelings locked up inside. Rather than verbalize them, we practice peace at any price. This compromises the unity and intimacy in our marriage. Denise and Frank suffered a breakdown in their communication. Denise was not entirely blameless. She had been so devastated by her prior failed relationship that she was afraid of being totally open and honest with Frank. She felt that he might leave her, which Frank would have never done. Frank had not been nurturing an atmosphere of love, equality, and respect to allow Denise to show her vulnerability in that area. He thought that he was being a perfect husband in every way, but he was not perfect. In actuality, he was being arrogant and self-absorbed when he had told himself he would never be those things.

In his apology, Frank asked for mercy. Denise saw his vulnerability and showed it to him. They became even closer than they were before. A skeleton in the closet had been removed, showing that a marriage is constant work whether you are married a year or 27 years. Picture it as a dull piece of soft bronze. Over the years, hopefully the bronze gradually gets shinier. Occasionally, it gets scuffed up and some of the shine gets rubbed off. Gradually, with time and the right attention to detail, it gets firmer and shinier and it almost looks like gold. If you don't pay attention to the scuff marks, the bronze loses the shine it has and becomes softer, eventually breaking apart. To break apart is an all too common occurrence in society today. However, it need not happen.

CHAPTER 8 QUESTIONS

1) In what ways did Frank and Denise use the marriage principles successfully?

_____

_____

_____

_____

2) Do you agree that even the best marriages are imperfect? Why?

_____

_____

_____

_____

3) In what ways could you sense Frank and Denise's love and affection? How did they show it?

_____

_____

_____

_____

4) In what ways do you see Frank and Denise sharing love and friendship? How does this make you feel?

_____

_____

_____

_____

CHAPTER 9

BEST FRIENDS AGAIN

As John Gottman's research has proven, "A more profound friendship will be a powerful shield against conflict" (40). What does being or having a best friend mean to you? Have you thought about your partner as a best friend? Do you like each other? Do you cherish each other? These are great questions to ask yourselves about each other. My partner is my best friend. What that means is that no matter what, I know she has my back. No matter what, means that there is an intense commitment that feels indestructible. This of course has been built from mutual affection, respect, trust, and intimacy.

We have to be cognizant now more than ever about affection and respect for each other. We live in a society that is dependent on cell phones or outside stimuli to keep us entertained 24/7. There are lots of distractions that go on in our daily lives. There needs to be a conscious effort by each partner to focus on connecting with each other on a daily basis. I would like to propose the idea of what I like to call a *Love Huddle*. A love huddle consists of choosing a time every day to come together in love to discuss each other's day. It is a time of connection. If you have something on your mind that needs to be talked about, take turns sharing. The goal of the love huddle is to build intimacy. What does it mean to build intimacy? It is a time to ask questions in order to know each other more deeply. That takes courage. From courage to being our true authentic selves, the love huddle becomes the vehicle by which trust and intimacy builds. Use love huddle time to share qualities that you love and admire about each other as well as any conflicts that may be happening in your lives. This love huddle should not be used exclusively to be a gripe session nor a promise for sex, but rather, a communication session created to build trust and love for each other. If sex happens, enjoy it. The love huddle requires us to risk vulnerability, but that is how true love and true joy in our relationship is built. You will see. Coming together in a love huddle with the intension of growing your relationship will break down walls that may be dividing you. Agree to one question you will ask each other. Take 10-15 minutes to write your answers down. When you are finished writing, exchange papers and read what your partner has written. The best way to do this is to answer the question with as many words as possible to express your true feelings. Rate each feeling from one to ten to describe the strength of the feeling. Next, describe your feeling as a taste, smell, touch, place, image, sound, color, or nature scene and describe why you have that feeling.

To give you an idea of how this works, let's put this into practice. I'd like to share an example of a love huddle exchange between my wife and I. We do this in the privacy of our bedroom at night.

Question: What qualities do I love most about you today?

Dr. Jeep to Vanessa:

Honey,

The quality that I appreciate most about you is your love for me and our kids. I feel excited about this like when I was waiting in line in Toronto at the Pantages Theatre knowing I was about to ask you to marry me, or like in Paris at the Eiffel Tower as I was waiting to give you your 10 year anniversary ring knowing you had no idea that was about to happen. The feeling is a 10 out of 10. If the feeling was a smell, it would be the sweet smell of a rose. The quality that I like about us the most is that we enjoy being together and we value our relationship first above all else. Writing this to you, I feel absolutely blessed. If this feeling was a color, it would be bright sunshine like the beach at Labadie while drinking rum punch and relaxing. If it was a touch, it would be like when you rub or scratch my back. If it was an image, it would be the blessing I felt when you had Quinn sing "Only God Could Love You More" at our wedding when I had a huge tear running down my cheek. If it were a nature scene it would be like watching the moon at midnight off the coast of Scandinavia when we were on top of the ship. I was feeling how incredibly lucky I was to be there with you experiencing that together.

All my love,

Jeep

Vanessa to Dr. Jeep:

My dearest Jeepie,

The qualities I most appreciate about you are your faithfulness, gentleness, and kindness. How do I feel as I write this to you? I feel peaceful, secure, and loved. I would say that my feelings are a 10 out of 10. To explain it as a sensation would be like when we are laying in each other's arms totally at peace and relaxed drinking in the feeling as if it were a smooth, sweet wine we're sipping on. If it were a smell, I would describe it as lavender. Fresh, calm, and relaxed. A nature scene would have us out in the middle of the vast ocean together on a ship in the hot tub, floating and enjoying the moon and stars and our together-ness. The quality in us that I appreciate the most is our commitment to our marriage and to each other. I feel a strong 10. The feeling is much like Sami (our dog) when she feels safe enough to lay on the floor and not move when we walk by because she trusts we won't step on her. The taste would be Sarris' chocolate pretzels. I am the salt and you are the sweet chocolate, and it is a perfect match. They go together so smoothly. The voice of my feeling would shout, "As a child, this is exactly what I dreamed of having in my marriage with my spouse!" I hit the jackpot with you, my Jeepie.

I love you deeply,

V.

* * *

As you can see, we use descriptive words to convey our feelings. We are painting the picture for our partner to see, touch, smell, taste, and feel. This communication engages all of our senses and touches our souls.

I gave an example of a positive question. However, if there is an issue between the two of you that needs to be fixed, this provides a better form of communication. We are taking the time to think it out by writing it. The description of negative feelings is less threatening when they are written. They can be communicated in a kinder and gentler way. As John Gottman says, "Although it is stressful to listen to your partner's negative feelings, remember that successful relationships live by the motto: 'When you're in pain, the world stops and I listen.' This is even true when your partner's anger, sadness, disappointment, or fear is directed at you" (40). I will attest to the fact that arguments can get very heated and emotional when we don't take our disagreement to the love huddle. Instead it becomes a shouting match. At times, if I feel that I am right, I dig my heals in to make my point. By the time I get to that part in a disagreement, I'm out to win! So instead of us zeroing in on what our argument is about, we are fighting to win. I can tell you from experience that it is better for our relationship if we go straight to the feelings. We can more fully express our feelings by writing rather then speaking. Through writing, we communicate our feelings without a tone of voice or facial expressions that can be misinterpreted by our partner. Writing is non-threatening. We defuse our emotions through writing and learn that no one is right. We must discuss the disagreement and work on a solution that we are both comfortable with.

The topics in disagreements are most often related to money, sex, kids, work stress, and housework according to John Gottman's research (40). Remember the Golden Rule: treat your spouse as you want to be treated.

Some questions to explore in the love huddle might be:

- What is the most vulnerable thing I should share with you today?
- How do I feel when I have sex when I don't want to?
- How do I like you to touch me?
- Is our marriage bed sacred?

- How do I feel when you say no?
- What do you love the most about me?
- What about you excites me the most?

We have used this technique in our relationship when we have differences in intimacy (both physically and emotionally), finances, and family. This technique allows me to really sense how my wife feels and how deeply she feels it. It allows me to dial right into that feeling and truly understand her.

There are endless possibilities with questions. If you would like more ideas, please visit our website at: www. bestfriendsagain.com. Dr. Jeep can be reached for couple's coaching consultations through his website.

EPILOGUE
WHAT'S FOREVER FOR?

Michael Martin Murphey recorded the song "What's Forever For" in 1982 (41). I cannot think of a better title for this book. It is absolutely what my book is about—the quality of our marriage preparation, the seriousness of our marriage vows, and the principles we use to keep our love alive during the difficult times. No one is exempt from hard times. The hard times test the strength of our marriage. Strength builds when we take a risk and become vulnerable through open and honest communication. When we trust in our love and this process, we enjoy the fruits of our labor—unity and true joy.

As I discussed earlier, the statistics about marriage failure are daunting and the data regarding relationships even ending up in marriage is discouraging. Marriage is at the heart of our society and its success or failure says a lot about where we are as a culture. According to *The Amazing Advantages of a Nuclear Family*, "Familial relationships and the family environment play an important role in the holistic and integrated development of the individual as well as how the individual will function and behave in society" (42).

It is through the example of the mother, father, and siblings that children learn how to become responsible members of society. They learn about relationships, productivity, and responsibility through interactions with and the examples of their parents and siblings.

Broken marriages, in my opinion and in those of others, are responsible for many of the problems society is experiencing today. Many children come from broken families, so they lack role models. In lacking proper direction, they can become associated with people who are not productive and responsible members of society. The Declaration of Independence provides for "Life, Liberty, and the pursuit of Happiness," but it does not guarantee it (43). Children of successful, loving, and caring families have a better ability to pursue those ideals.

By not learning the basic values required to become responsible members of society, children risk not prospering or surviving in today's dog-eat-dog world. Again, as the lyrics in the song "What's Forever For" say, "... lately all I've been seeing are people throwing love away and losing their minds" (41). We live in a society that has changed the focus from we to me. Fighting to save a rocky, troubled relationship has become not worth it to many. It's about what's best for me not we. Marriages are discarded too easily because it's simpler to quit rather than fight. Sadly, many couples who go down this road don't foresee the consequences to themselves and their children. It is in essence, "losing your mind" when spouses realize what they could've had if they'd tried harder. Mr. Murphey goes on to say, "I see love hungry people tryin' their best to survive, while in their head they dream of romance, if they can keep it alive" (41). That pretty much says it all.

I have tried to champion marriage in this book. It is my hope that the example of the three marriages that I have thoroughly reviewed with you will serve as a guide for what works and what does not work in marriage. Hopefully, the three generations of marriages have shown the different trials and tribulations of each generation and how they were handled. There are differences in what each generation faces but many challenges are still the same.

Think back to a time when you were in love. To love and to be loved is perhaps one of the greatest joys in life! Love as well as empathy, vulnerability, kindness, and compassion are the keys to success in any marriage. Spouses must have an altruistic sense of their marriage. That is to say they must understand that the success of their marriage as a whole is more important than their own desires.

In closing, St. Paul says in 1 Corinthians 13:4-8, 13: "Love is patient, love is kind. It does not envy, it does not boast, it is not proud. It does not dishonor others, it is not self-seeking, it is not easily angered, it keeps no record of wrongs. Love does not delight in evil but rejoices with the truth. It always protects, always trusts, always hopes, always perseveres. Love never fails... And now these three remain: faith, hope and love. But the greatest of these is love" (44).

BIBLIOGRAPHY

1) www.onlythebible.com/Poems/Footprints-in-the-Sand-Poem.html

2) www.webmd.com/healthy-aging/features/importance-of-marriage#1

3) www.heritage.org/marriage-and-family/report/the-necessity-marriage

4) Yalith Wijesurendra. *Buddhist Answers: for the Critical Questions: A Bridge from Religion to Science and Reason.*

5) https://christianity.org.uk/article/a-christian-view-of-marriage

6) www.mormonbeliefs.org/mormon-beliefs-marriage

7) www.learnreligions.com/the–sacrament–of–marriage-542134

8) www.biblegateway.com/passage/?search=James+3%3A5-6&version=NIV

9) www.merriam-webster.com/dictionary/word?src=search-dict-box

10) www.dailyjournal.net/2016/10/08/whats_needed_in_an_uncivil_world_thumpers_rule/

11) www.goodreads.com/quotes/55805-remember-not-only-to-say-the-right-thing-in-the#:~:text=Quotes%20%3E%20Quotable%20Quote-,%E2%80%9CRemember%20not%20only%20to%20say%20the%20right%20thing%20

in%20the,thing%20at%20the%20tempting%20 moment.%E2%80%9D

12) https://m.huffpost.com/us/entry/us_6324786

13) https://stacywestfall.com/t-h-i-n-k-before-you-speak-written-by-jesse-westfall/

14) www.inspiringquotes.us/quotes/SfnH_62tsqgBx

15) www.biblegateway.com/passage/?search=2+Thessalonians+3%#A13&version=NIV

16) www.dictionary.com/browse/humility?s=t

17) www.dictionary.com/browse/arrogance?s=t

18) www.guruhabits.com/rules-for-fair-productive-argument

19) www.biblegateway.com/passage/?search=Matthew+18%3A22&version=NIV

20) www.dictionary.com/browse/vulnerability#

21) www.goodreads.com/book/show/23500254-the-power-of-vulnerability

22) www.dictionary.com/browse/entrenchment?s=t

23) www.biblegateway.com/passage/?search=Matthew+6%3A15&version=NIV

24) www.biblegateway.com/passage/?search=Mark+10%3A8&version=NIV

25) www.bmj.com/content/350/bmj.h706

26) www.webmd.com/mental-health/news/20180508/doctors-suicide-rate-highest-of-any-profession#1

27) https://lendedu.com/blog/average-medical-school-debt/#:~:text=While%20some%20

lucky%20students%20might%20receive%20
scholarships%20or,balance%20for%20gradu-
ating%20students%20in%202018%20was%20
%24196%2C520

28) www.biblegateway.com/
passage/?search=John+15%3A13&version=NIV

29) www.biblegateway.com/passage/?-
search=Song+of+Solomon+3%3A4&version=NIV

30) www.si.com/mlb/2009/07/05/gehrig-text

31) www.biblegateway.com/passage/?-
search=Song+of+Solomon+6%3A3&version=NIV

32) www.biblegateway.com/
passage/?search=Matthew+19%3A5&version=NIV

33) www.dictionary.com/browse/empathetic?s=t

34) www.dictionary.com/browse/indifference#

35) www.cybersalt.org/quotes/quote-1773

36) www.biblegateway.com/passage/?search=Philippi-
ans+2%3A3&version=NIV

37) www.biblegateway.com/passage/?search=prov-
erbs+21%3A04&version=NIV

38) www.biblegateway.com/
passage/?search=John+14%3A27&version=NIV

39) www.webmd.com/depression/features/postpartum

40) John Gottman. *The 7 Principles to Making Marriage
Work.*

41) www.songlyrics.com/micheal-martin-murphey/
what-s-forever-for-lyrics/

42) www.icytales.com/advantages-of-a-nuclear-family
43) http://founding.com/the-declaration/founding-principles/among-these-are-life-liberty-and-the-pursuit-of-happiness
44) www.biblegateway.com/passage/?search=1+Corinthians+13%3A4-13&version=NIV

ABOUT THE AUTHOR

Dr. George "Jeep" Naum has always been passionate about helping, teaching, and educating others. He has served as a doctor for 30 years and as a coach for engaged and married couples for over 25 years.

Dr. Jeep earned his bachelor of science in zoology at Marshall University, his doctor of osteopathic medicine at West Virginia School of Osteopathic Medicine, his family practice specialty degree at The Medical Center of Beaver, Pennsylvania, and his certification and fellowship at the American Academy of Family Physicians. He is devoted to many causes, including Catholic Charities, Meals on Wheels of the Upper Ohio Valley, and St. Michael's Catholic Church.

Dr. Jeep enjoys sports and traveling. He and his soulmate, Vanessa, have been happily and successfully married since 1992. Together they have three children and currently reside in Wheeling, West Virginia.

To connect, email him at drjeep13@yahoo.com

purposely created

PUBLISHING

CREATING DISTINCTIVE BOOKS
WITH INTENTIONAL RESULTS

We're a collaborative group of creative masterminds
with a mission to produce high-quality books to position
you for monumental success in the marketplace.

Our professional team of writers, editors, designers,
and marketing strategists work closely together to ensure
that every detail of your book is a clear representation
of the message in your writing.

Want to know more?
Write to us at info@publishyourgift.com
or call (888) 949-6228

Discover great books, exclusive offers, and more at
www.PublishYourGift.com

Connect with us on social media

@publishyourgift